Charles Dickens'

A TALE OF TWO CITIES

HENRY I. HUBERT
DEPARTMENT OF ENGLISH
UNIVERSITY OF KENTUCKY

Simon & Schuster, Inc.
15 Columbus Circle
New York, NY 10023

Monarch and colophons are trademarks
of Simon & Schuster, registered in the
U.S. Patent and Trademark Office.

ISBN: 0-671-00611-8

Library of Congress Catalog Card Number: 65-7291

Printed in the United States of America

CONTENTS

one   *THE AUTHOR: CHARLES DICKENS*   **5**

        The life of Charles Dickens; his work,
          and influences on his writing

two   *THE BOOK: A TALE OF TWO CITIES*   **9**

        Brief summary of the plot   *9*

        Detailed summary with analytic comment   *14*

three   *THE CHARACTERS*   **82**

        Description and analysis of the characters

four   *COMMENTARY*   **86**

        Analysis of Dickens' style and technique

five   *TEST QUESTIONS*   **91**

        Essay questions and detailed answers

six   *FURTHER READING*   **95**

        A bibliography for the author and his works,
          and a guide to further research

INTRODUCTION

THE LIFE OF CHARLES DICKENS

EARLY LIFE. Charles Dickens was born on February 7, 1812 in Land-port, Portsea, England, to John and Elizabeth Dickens, and was christened Charles John Huffham Dickens. Dickens' father was a clerk in the British Navy Pay Office in Portsea. John Dickens was always in debt and this kept the family moving from one lodging to another, each more squalid than the one before. Dickens had seven sisters and brothers — one older than himself, Fanny, and six younger, two of whom died in childhood.

Charles was a frail child and he became bookish early. Among the works he read as a boy were "Roderick Random," "Peregrine Pickle," "Humphrey Clinker," "Tom Jones," "The Vicar of Wakefield," "Don Quixote," "Gil Blas," "Robinson Crusoe," "The Arabian Nights," and "Tales of the Genii." In his early years, when the family was living at Chatham, he attended something like a school run by some women in the district; at ages eight and nine he attended something closer to a real school kept by a William Giles, a Baptist minister.

HIS FATHER'S IMPRISONMENT. In 1821, John Dickens moved his family to London, having been reassigned there by the British Admiralty. In London, Dickens experienced the darkest period of his childhood. The family lived in desperate circumstances as John Dickens sank deeper and deeper into debt. Finally, John Dickens was thrown into Marshaisea Prison as a debtor, and shortly after Mrs. Dickens and the children were forced to move into the prison with him, Mrs. Dickens being unable to support herself and the children. Work was found for Charles as a label-paster at a blacking factory. He found a small room nearby and lived there, visiting the prison on Sundays. The job was a sordid one and his companions were of the lowest type. Charles hated his situation and lived in misery during this time. At one point, his father had an argument with the relative who employed young Charles, and John Dickens withdrew his son from the job. Charles was greatly relieved. His mother, however, attempted to patch up the differences which had caused the argument so that Charles might return to work. Though she was unsuccessful, Charles remembered this attempt, indignantly, for the rest of his life.

BETTER DAYS. Finally, a small legacy enabled the Dickens family to leave prison, and after much moving about in London, Charles, from ages twelve to fourteen, finally went to a standard school — the Wellington House Academy. At fourteen, he became an attorney's clerk, what we would call an office boy, and here began his first study of the law, which would lead to his great knowledge of the subject and his even greater contempt for it, as is shown in his works. At this time, Dickens' father became a reporter for a London newspaper in the press gallery of the House of Commons. For this job Dickens had to learn shorthand and before long his son mastered it, too. Also at this time, Charles became interested in the theater and he took to organizing amateur theatrical performances. It was an interest which would never leave him.

FIRST WRITINGS. Charles was admitted as a reporter to the House of Commons in 1831 at the age of nineteen. He was a skilled shorthand reporter and he had begun to write. At school he had improvised dramas and characters; now, he started writing stories. He sent a story to the *Old Monthly Magazine* which was accepted for publication, and, shortly after, nine other works by him appeared there. Since there was no pay for these items, Dickens then stopped contributing. Then, the newspaper for which Charles was working, *The Morning Chronicle,* started an evening edition. Dickens made the suggestion that he contribute "sketches" and be paid for them, in addition to his regular salary as a reporter. The suggestion was accepted and Dickens began writing sketches for the *Evening Chronicle* under the pen-name of "Boz," a name which became well-known to the newspaper's readers. In 1836 these "Sketches by Boz" appeared in book form, illustrated by the prominent artist, George Cruikshank.

MARRIAGE AND SUCCESS. The manager of the *Evening Chronicle* was a man named Hogarth and he had three beautiful daughters. Charles became friendly with the family and would often visit their home. Dickens became engaged to one of the daughters, Catherine Hogarth, and on April 2, 1836, two days after the appearance of the first installment of his new work, "Pickwick Papers," Catherine Hogarth and Charles Dickens were married. "The Posthumous Papers of the Pickwick Club," to give the work its full title, was published in a magazine during 1836 and 1837. It is important to remember that almost all of Dickens' works were first published in installments in various periodicals and only appeared in book form after the serialization was complete. This factor necessarily placed restrictions on Dickens as to content and form. The first installment of "Pickwick" was not a success, but by the fourth installment sales had leaped, and by its completion the novel had repaid the publishers handsomely, bringing them profits of over 20,000 pounds (the equivalent today of $56,000 and a good deal m re at that time).

Life at this time was serene for Charles Dickens. He was happily married and he was having his first success as an author. He bought a house for his parents, and during the years 1837-1839, three children were born to Charles and Catherine Dickens: Mary, Kate, and Walter. At this period in his life, Dickens met John Forster, who served him as friend, biographer, executor, and proofreader.

With fame and wealth came many offers of employment. He accepted the post of Editor for a new magazine called *Bentley's Miscellany*. It was in this publication that "Oliveer Twist" first appeared, as well as several other works. His interest in the theater caused him to write four plays, three of which were performed (the manuscripts were later lost, and Dickens was reportedly glad they were).

A RESPECTED AUTHOR. His income continuing to rise, Charles bought a large house for himself and his family and a little country house for his parents. He lived like a lord, and he continued turning out works one after the other, as well as taking on other assignments. In 1838, there appeared "Nicholas Nickleby," illustrated by Hablot Browne (who signed himself "Phiz"), and it was very successful. Then "Master Humphrey's Clock" (unsuccessful) and "The Old Curiosity Shop" and "Barnaby Rudge" (both successful) appeared. England then began to honor Dickens, and on a trip through Scotland in 1841 he was cheered by the populace, given testimonial dinners, and even offered a political post, which he refused.

FIRST TRIP TO AMERICA. In 1842, Dickens came to America. His reputation had preceded him and the country went wild over this great English man of letters. At first Dickens was very pleased with the United States, but his first look at slavery changed his attitude, and his constant references to the need for an international copyright agreement in his speeches annoyed some of his listeners (at that time there was no such agreement and Dickens' works were published here with no royalty payment to the author). Finally, he became disenchanted and returned to England in June, 1842.

Soon, two more children were born, Francis and Alfred, and there appeared "American Notes," "Martin Chuzzlewit," and "A Christmas Carol." "American Notes" and, particularly, "Martin Chuzzlewit" were badly received in America. "Chuzzlewit" was a parody and a strong criticism of American civilization. Dickens thought of the idea for "A Christmas Carol" while working on "Nicholas Nickleby." He became absorbed in it, and when it appeared there was a very sympathetic reception for it, though it was not a financial success.

HEIGHT OF FAME WITH "COPPERFIELD".   In 1844, the Dickens family went on a tour of Europe. In December of that year, Dickens returned to London for a brief time, and during this visit gave a reading of a short story of his, "The Chimes," for some friends. Then he returned to Europe to join his family. In 1845 the family returned to London, and in the next three years there appeared two more works: "Dombey and Son," and "David Copperfield," the latter considered by many to be Dickens' greatest work. With its publication Dickens achieved the height of his fame. He himself called it his favorite book. It was written at the age of thirty-seven, when he was happy and prosperous, and one has the feeling that it flowed from his pen onto the paper.

A new newspaper was then set up in London, the *Daily News,* and Dickens became editor-in-chief at 2000 pounds a year. But Dickens tired of the enterprise in a week and resigned in three. The paper was to go on to become a very influential journal. During this time, Dickens continued dabbling in amateur theatricals. Soon, three more children were born: Sampson, Sydney, and Henry.

NEW EDITORIAL DUTIES.   In 1850, Dickens took on the editorial labors of *Household Words* and he was to continue as an editor, until his death, on this publication and another, *All the Year Round.* In 1851, John Dickens died, but he and Mrs. Dickens were to live on in the works of their son as Mr. Micawber (in "David Copperfield") and Mrs. Nickleby. The year 1851 also saw the appearance of "A Child's History of England" and the settling of the Dickens family in a new home, where Dickens began writing "Bleak House." In 1852, another son was born: Edmund. In 1853, "Bleak House" was completed and was an overwhelming success. In this same year, Dickens gave the first public reading from his works at Birmingham which was to lead to another career for him.

BREAKUP OF DICKENS' MARRIAGE.   During these years Dickens' domestic situation began to collapse. He had seen it coming for a long time, but the strain became greater at this period of his life, with his many irons in the fire. "Hard Times" appeared in 1854 and was a total failure. It was followed by "Little Dorrit" in 1856, also a failure. In 1858, he and his wife separated. There is little known about his marriage, for it never served as a source for his works, as far as we know, although Dickens drew upon everything else he saw and experienced for his characters and plots. The separation, on top of the strains of overwork, shook Dickens' composure and he lashed out in print at several people he was certain were wronging him. He threw himself, then, into giving professional readings. These were extremely well-received, but Dickens was taking on too much. Writing, editing, giving readings, and engaging in amateur theatricals — these were to impair his health as well as upset his mental poise.

FIRST APPEARANCE OF "A TALE OF TWO CITIES". After having a falling-out with the publishers of *Household Words*, Dickens began a new magazine called *All the Year Round*, which was published by Chapman and Hall. In the opening number he began "A Tale of Two Cities." He had chosen the title in March, 1859 and the book appeared in installments from April through November, 1859. It was the last of Dickens' works to be illustrated by "Phiz," for Dickens had, for some reason, broken off the relationship with the artist Browne.

LAST YEARS. The next few years were filled to overflowing with activity. His tours took up a larger part of his life. He returned to the United States and visited Canada, reading from his works. Everywhere lines formed to hear him. He was lionized by everyone and, both artistically and financially, the readings were a tremendous success. He continued writing, producing "Great Expectations" and "Our Mutual Friend," as well as several lesser works.

On June 9th, 1870, wihle working on "The Mystery of Edwin Drood" in London, Dickens died. He was mourned by a grateful nation, and was buried alongside England's other great writers in Westminster Abbey in London.

A BRIEF SYNOPSIS OF THE PLOT OF

"A TALE OF TWO CITIES"

Mr. Jarvis Lorry, a representative of Tellson's Bank in London, is sent by his firm on a mission to Paris. The mission is to meet a newly-released prisoner of the Bastille, Doctor Alexandre Manette, in Paris and to bring him back to London to be cared for by his daughter, Lucie Manette. Lucie has lived in ignorance of her father's existence and Mr. Lorry is to meet her at Dover and break the news to her.

The two meet; Lucie is informed that her father is alive, which news awakens fear and trepidation in her breast, and the two journey to Paris. They proceed to a wine shop in the Saint Antoine region and there they meet Ernest Defarge, keeper of the wine shop and a former servant of Dr. Manette's. Defarge has been caring for the doctor pending the arrival of Lucie and Mr. Lorry. The Shopkeeper takes them to a garret room where they see an old, white-haired man making shoes: it is Doctor Manette, who took up the trade in prison and who now thinks of himself only as a shoemaker, having forgotten his earlier existence. After an emotional scene between father and daughter, during which there is a brief flicker of remembrance in the doctor's eyes, arrangements are made for the three to leave Paris immediately. In a short while Defarge bids goodbye to them as the coach sets out for Calais with its three passengers, on the first leg of the trip to London.

The second book opens five years later. During this time, Dr. Manette has been restored to his old self through Lucie's tender care and father and daughter live in a modest lodging, with Miss Pross, Lucie's old nurse, as maid and general housekeeper. There Dr. Manette carries on a small medical practice. One day, Jerry Cruncher, a messenger for Tellson's Bank, is told to go to the Old Bailey, London's Criminal Courts Building, to await a message from Mr. Lorry who is there. Jerry proceeds to the Old Bailey and finds a treason trial in progress. The accused, Charles Darnay, is called a spy for France and several witnesses appear, including Mr. Lorry, Dr. Manette and Lucie, all of whom met Darnay on the packet boat sailing from Calais to Dover on that night five years ago when Dr. Manette was brought to London. Things look dark for Darnay, but Mr. Stryver, Darnay's counsel, manages to blacken the characters of two of the witnesses and Stryver's assistant, Sydney Carton, upsets the testimony of a third by calling Stryver's attention to a striking resemblance between himself, Carton, and the prisoner Darnay. Darnay is acquitted. While Darnay is being congratulated after the trial, a look of fear and doubt crosses Dr. Manette's face as if an old memory was awakened by Darnay.

At this time in France, the clouds of the coming revolution continue to darken the skies as the downtrodden peasants work and starve to fatten the coffers of the nobility. One nobleman, a Marquis, on his way home from a lavish ball, crushes a child beneath the wheels of his coach and is quite unconcerned about it, tossing a gold coin to the stricken father. That evening, the Marquis receives a visitor at his chateau: his nephew, Charles Darnay, who has come once again to attempt to persuade his uncle to improve the lot of the peasantry, but with no success. Later in the evening, the Marquis is slain in his bed and the clouds of revolution grow blacker in the night sky.

Both Charles Darnay and Sydney Carton have fallen in love with Lucie Manette on the occasion of her appearance at Darnay's trial. Carton, who is a slovenly, debauched man, knows that it would be fruitless to woo Lucie, but he visits her and pledges her his eternal friendship and devotion. Darnay approaches Dr. Manette to reveal his love for Lucie. Dr. Manette is visibly disturbed by this news of Darnay's affection for his daughter, but promises to give his blessing to a marriage if Lucie should express her love for Darnay.

A new royal spy is commissioned for the Saint Antoine quarter of Paris. It is John Barsad, who was one of the witnesses at Darnay's trial. The word travels rapidly to the wine shop and to the ears of Monsieur and Madame Defarge, leaders of the underground conspiracy which will soon give the signal for revolution. Barsad arrives at the wine shop to try to get some information concerning the unrest of the peasantry, but the Defarges give nothing away. Only when he reveals the news that Lucie is to wed Charles Darnay, nephew of the murdered Marquis, does Defarge show any emotion. The spy makes a mental note of this and leaves.

Lucie's wedding day arrives and, as had been agreed beforehand, Darnay reveals his true identity to Dr. Manette before the ceremony. Then Lucie and Charles are married and they leave on their honeymoon. Darnay's revelation has a serious effect on Dr. Manette and he loses his stability and once again becomes a shoemaker. After nine days, however, he recovers with no seeming ill effects, and as he goes off to join Lucie and Charles, Mr. Lorry and Miss Pross destroy his shoemaking equipment. Sydney Carton arrives at the house shortly after the Darnays' return and asks Darnay if they can be friends, to which request Darnay assents heartily. Meanwhile, the situation in France has worsened and many nobles are fleeing France for their lives, taking whatever valuables they can with them or having them sent to England. Mr. Lorry is kept busy at the bank, for Tellson's has a French office and does much business with its French customers. Mr. Lorry is asked by the bank to return to Paris once more to try to straighten out the bank's affairs there, which are in chaos. On the day of his departure, he and Charles Darnay are conversing at Tellson's when a letter is brought. It is addressed to the Marquis Saint Evrémonde, Charles' true name, which has been concealed from everyone except Dr. Manette. Darnay takes the letter and promises to deliver it. Later, he reads it and learns that it is from a representative of his in France who has been arrested by the new Revolutionary government, and whose life is threatened for being a representative of a hated nobleman. Darnay resolves to return to Paris to save the man's life. He leaves London that night and finally reaches Paris. Upon his arrival in Paris, he is thrown into prison. Dr. Manette and Lucie, along with Miss Pross and little Lucie, ruch to Paris when they hear of Charles' fate. Dr. Manette, as a former prisoner in the Bastille, has great influence with the Revolutionary government and he manages to keep Charles safe though he is unable to arrange his releave. The prisoners, meanwhile, are being slaughtered in droves. Finally, many months later, Darnay is brought to trial and, through Dr. Manette's influence, is released. Darnay returns to Lucie's loving arms, but within twenty-four hours he is arrested again: this time accused by the Defarges and one other person. At the trial, the one other person turns out to be Dr. Manette himself, and the cause of Darnay's arrest is an old diary the doctor wrote while he was in prison and which was found by Defarge on the day the Bastille fell. In this diary Dr. Manette cursed the Evrémonde family for causing his imprisonment, and Charles Darnay, as the last living descendant of the family of Saint Evrémonde, is thus cursed by the doctor as well. Darnay is sentenced to die within twenty-four hours. Dr. Manette attempts once again to have him released, but to no avail. But Sydney Carton, who has arrived in Paris, conceives a scheme to spare Darnay's life. He forces John Barsad, who is now a spy for the prisons, to aid him in the scheme. He manages to visit Darnay's cell, change clothes with the prisoner, drug him, and have him taken out by Barsad to a coach, where Mr. Lorry is waiting with Lucie and Dr. Manette. Carton remains in the cell in Darnay's place.

As the prisoners who are to be executed assemble, Carton answers to the name Saint Evrémonde, and he proceeds to the place of execution and there is slain in place of Charles Darnay to fulfill his pledge to Lucie. Madame Defarge, meanwhile, in her hatred for the Saint Evrémonde family, decides that the whole family must be wiped out and, accordingly, she proceeds to Lucie's lodgings. However, only Miss Pross is there, and in a struggle between the two women, Madame Defarge is killed, while the people who were the objects of her hatred flee to England and safety.

THE WORKS OF CHARLES DICKENS

Sketches by Boz. 1835-36
Sunday Under Three Heads, etc. 1836
Village Coquettes, comic opera. 1836
The Strange Gentleman, comic burletta. 1837
Is She His Wife? or Something Singular, comic burletta. Acted 1837.
Posthumous Papers of the Pickwick Club. 1836-37
Mudfog Papers. 1837-39
Memoirs of Joseph Grimaldi, edited by Boz. 1838
Oliver Twist, or The Parish Boy's Progress. 1838
Sketches of Young Gentlemen. 1838
Life and Adventures of Nicholas Nickleby. 1838-39
Sketches of Young Couples, etc. 1840
Master Humphrey's Clock, The Old Curiosity Shop, Barnaby Rudge.
    1840-41
American Notes. 1842

A Christmas Carol in Prose. 1843
Life and Adventures of Martin Chuzzlewit. 1843-44
The Chimes. 1844
The Cricket on the Hearth. 1845
Pictures from Italy. 1846
The Battle of Life. 1846
Dealings with the Firm of Dombey and Son. 1846-48
The Haunted Man, and the Ghost's Bargain. 1848
The Personal History of David Copperfield. 1849-50
Christmas Stories. 1850-67
Bleak House. 1852-53
A Child's History of England. 1854
Hard Times for These Times. 1854
Little Dorrit. 1855-57
A Tale of Two Cities. 1859
Great Expectations. 1861
Our Mutual Friend. 1864-65
Religious Opinions of the late Rev. Chauncey Hate Townhend, ed.
    A.D. 1869
Landor's Life. 1870
Mystery of Edwin Drood (unfinished). 1870

THE CHARACTERS OF "A TALE OF TWO CITIES"

John Barsad, a spy and secret informer, first in London, later in Paris
Sydney Carton, a London barrister, assistant to Mr. Stryver
Roger Cly, an Old Bailey spy, friend of John Barsad
Jerry Cruncher, a messenger and odd-job man at Tellson's Bank
Mrs. Cruncher, Jerry's wife
Young Jerry Cruncher, son of the above.
Charles Darnay, an emigrant Frenchman, now living in London
Ernest Defarge, keeper of a wine-shop in Paris
Madame Thérèse Defarge, wife of Ernest Defarge
Théophile Gabelle, a postmaster and local functionary for the estate of
    Saint Evrémonde
Gaspard, a citizen of Paris
Jacques One
Jacques Two
Jacques Three
Revolutionists, associates of Ernest Defarge
Jacques Four, a name assumeed by Ernest Defarge
Jacques Five, a mender of roads, afterward a wood-sawyer
Mr. Jarvis Lorry, a representative of Tellson's Bank and friend of the
    Manettes

Dr. Alexandre Manette, a physician of Paris, imprisoned for many
    years in the Bastille

Lucie Manette, daughter of Dr. Manette

Miss Pross, maid to Lucie Manette

Marquis Saint Evrémonde — 1. — The former Marquis, now de-
    ceased, mentioned in Dr. Manette's story

Marquis Saint Evrémonde — 2. — The present Marquis

Marquise Saint Evrémonde, the wife of the former Marquis — 1. —,
    also mentioned in Dr. Manette's story

Mr. Stryver, a London barrister

The Vengeance, a leading woman Revolutionist in Paris

"A TALE OF TWO CITIES"

BOOK THE FIRST — RECALLED TO LIFE

CHAPTER 1.　THE PERIOD

"It was the best of times, it was the worst of times. . . ." With these
famous words Charles Dickens begins his novel of the French Revolution, "A Tale of Two Cities." In the opening chapter, Dickens re-
creates the mood of the times both in England and in France. In relating
and contrasting several news items of the day, he manages amazingly
well to capture the flavor and underlying unrest of both countries.

> **COMMENT:** Dickens deliberately adopts a dry, ironic tone in this
> opening chapter. In this manner the air of foreboding is made
> much more apparent to the reader, understatement making the hor-
> rible details even more horrible. The events in England that he
> mentions, such as the disinterest of the nobility where the common
> people are concerned and the lawlessness which permitted daring
> robberies in the heart of London, show that country to be in a
> chaotic state, internally. However, the events in France that he
> cites, such as the torture and death of a young man for not kneeling
> to a distant procession of monks, show the greater deterioration
> there, and herald the grim events which are to unfold in France
> during the years to come in the telling of this story.

CHAPTER 2.　THE MAIL

The coach which delivers the mail between London and Dover is laboring up Shooter's Hill through the mud with its contents. Beside it, to ease
the strain on the horses, walk its three passengers while the coachman

and a guard sit atop the coach. With highwaymen being common in those days no one trusts anyone else. Thus, each passenger keeps to himself and doesn't become friendly with the others for fear of giving out information which might make him a likely target for a robber; and the guard is suspicious of them all.

As the coach reaches the summit of the hill and pauses for the passengers to reclaim their seats, a horseman is heard approaching. Fear overcomes the passengers as the guard shouts out to the unseen horseman to halt. After stating his business, the horseman is permitted to approach while the guard stands warily with his gun at the ready. The rider is Jerry Cruncher, a messenger from the venerable London bank of Tellson's with a message from Mr. Jarvis Lorry, a representative of the bank who is a passenger in the coach and who is bound for Paris. The message reads "Wait at Dover for Mam'selle." In reply, Mr. Lorry gives Jerry the message, "Recalled to life." The coach rumbles on its way again while the coachman and guard puzzle over the reply. As the sounds of the coach fade in the distance, Jerry, left on the road, also considers Mr. Lorry's reply, but can make no sense of it. He decides that he, Jerry, would be in a "blazing bad way if recalling to life was to come into fashion."

> **COMMENT:**   In this chapter we are introduced to the first of the many important characters we are to meet in the course of the story: Mr. Jarvis Lorry, an old, reliable, somewhat stuffy member of the firm of Tellson's, a "man of business," as he is fond of calling himself, who is to set so many things into motion through his meeting with "Mam'selle" at Dover. And we also meet Jerry Cruncher who serves as a messenger and odd-job man at Tellson's, but who, in the dark of night when off duty, works as "an honest tradesman," in his own words, at some mysterious trade whose devious aspects would indeed put him in a bad way if recalling to life was to come into fashion. The chapters devoted to Jerry Cruncher in this book are the closest we come to any comic relief. But the comic Jerry is to become, later, a great help to the others in the story, and his nocturnal prowling will provide a trump card in a crucial moment near the close of the book.

CHAPTER 3.   THE NIGHT SHADOWS

As Jerry Cruncher rides back to London, mulling over the message he is to deliver to Tellson's Bank, we find ourselves with Mr. Lorry in the coach rattling over the rough roads on the way to Dover, as he thinks about his reason for going to Paris: he is on his way to dig someone out of a grave. The dull rhythm of the coach causes him to nod, and in his mind he sees a multitude of faces, all worn and wasted, the hair prematurely white; and to Mr. Lorry's unspoken question, "Buried how long?" the answer comes, "Almost eighteen years." "I hope you care to live?" "I can't say." After such a dialogue, Mr. Lorry in his dream world begins to dig the spectre out of the earth; then he comes to himself and opens the window of the coach to let the wind and rain falling on his cheek bring him back to reality. But only for a short time, for before his mind's eye the image of the wasted face appears again, repeating the words, "Almost eighteen years," "I can't say," until Mr. Lorry finally awakes to find himself in the bright light of day and he marvels that a man who has been buried alive for eighteen years is about to be released.

COMMENT: Here we learn of Mr. Lorry's purpose in going to Paris: to meet and bring back to London one Doctor Alexandre Manette, a French physician who has been imprisoned in France for eighteen years under a "lettre de cachet," the infamous document on which a nobleman could write the name of anyone whom he wanted removed for personal reasons. A person so named could be consigned to prison without trial or accusation, often to die there, never knowing the name of his accuser or what he was accused of. The circumstances of Dr. Manette's imprisonment are to be told with dramatic effect later in the book.

CHAPTER 4. THE PREPARATION

The coach arrives at Dover and Mr. Lorry checks into the Royal George Hotel. After refreshing himself, he comes to the Coffee Room for his breakfast. Here we are given a description of him: orderly and methodical, a little vain, rosy cheeks, a face which has been trained over many years to look composed and reserved as befitted a member of Tellson's Bank. As his breakfast is brought, Mr. Lorry speaks to the servant. "I wish accommodation prepared for a young lady who may come here at any time today. She may ask for Mr. Jarvis Lorry, or she may only ask for a gentleman from Tellson's Bank. Please to let me know." After breakfast, Mr. Lorry spends the afternoon strolling on the beach of the fishing village of Dover.

In the evening, as he is finishing dinner, the arrival of a coach is heard and shortly thereafter Mr. Lorry meets "Mam'selle" in her apartment. It is Lucie Manette, daughter of Dr. Manette. She has been told to come to Dover where she would be met by an official of Tellson's Bank who would go with her to Paris on business concerning her father. "Sir, it was told me by the Bank that the gentleman would explain to me the details of the business, and that I must prepare myself to find them of a surprising nature. I have done my best to prepare myself, and I naturally have a strong and eager interest to know what they are." Mr. Lorry finds it difficult to begin. Lucie Manette was brought to England from France by Mr. Lorry after her mother's death and she has lived all her life thinking her father dead. It is Mr. Lorry's task to reveal to Lucie that her father is alive so that after bringing him back from France she may care for him and try to restore him to his old self after his long ordeal in prison; but it is essential that all this be done quickly and with utmost secrecy. Finally, Mr. Lorry relates all this to Lucie in the form of a story, but the parallels are too obvious to what she knows of her father's life and her great agitation as the story unfolds shakes Mr. Lorry's calm and reserved demeanor. "There, there, there! See now, see now! The best and the worst are known to you, now. You are well on your way to the poor wronged gentleman, and, with a fair sea voyage, and a fair land journey, you will soon be at his dear side." She replies in a whisper, "I have been free, I have been happy, yet his ghost has never haunted me!" As the full truth penetrates her mind, Lucie is so upset that she falls into a daze. Mr. Lorry, unaccustomed to dealing with such an eventuality, calls for help, at which a wild-looking red-haired woman rushes in to tend to Lucie and restore her to her former condition.

> COMMENT: Lucie Manette, "not more than seventeen years of age," beautiful, golden-haired, gentle, and wise beyond her years, here learns of the role she is to play in this drama. After Mr. Manette disappeared, Lucie's mother had frantically searched for word of him for two years, with no success, and so she had determined that her daughter would not know the strange circumstances surrounding the Doctor's disappearance. Thus, Lucie was raised thinking her father dead. When Lucie's mother died, Lucie became the ward of Tellson's Bank which had administered the affairs of the Manette family. Mr. Lorry was given the assignment of bringing her back to England. Miss Pross, the red-haired, wildlooking woman who answered Mr. Lorry's call for help, has been with Lucie since the girl was ten years old and serves as cook, maid, governess and confidant. She loves Lucie as if Lucie were her own daughter, and her love and devotion will be put to the supreme test near the close of the story.

CHAPTER 5.   THE WINE SHOP

A wine-shop in the Saint Antonne region of Paris. A wine cask has been accidentally dropped from a delivery cart and has shattered on the pavement. The event has drawn the attention of all within sight or hearing and a large crowd hurries to the scene to sop up the wine from the street, using whatever means available: hands, cups, even handkerchiefs which are dipped into a puddle of wine and squeezed dry into the mouths of small children. The scene acquires almost a holiday mood, for all these people who live on dry crusts of bread and a little water suddenly find themselves drinking wine and a spirit of camaraderie prevails — some shake hands, some drink healths to their neighbors, others embrace and dance in the street.

When the wine has all been gathered up, the people return to their tasks — a woman returns to a pot of hot ashes with which she has been trying to ease the pain of her starved, emaciated fingers and toes. The wasted, cadaverous faces disappear from the scene to return to the cellars and garrets from which they have come and gloom once again settles down over the street, a gloom more natural to it than sunshine. The red wine has stained the street and the clothes and faces and hands of the people who have tasted it. One tall citizen writes the word "blood" on a wall with his wine-soaked fingers.

> **COMMENT:** This scene effectively portrays the squalor and deprivation of the French people and the spilling of the wine has a double meaning: it shows that the people cannot be kept much longer from having the necessities of life of which they have been so long deprived; and the wine running in the streets points to the bloodbath which will in a few years engulf this street and all of France. The tall citizen will soon have occasion to bitterly remember his grim joke, and in his grief he is to commit one of the first overt acts that will soon plunge the French people irrevocably into much madness and bloodshed.

After the incident of the wine, we are given a further picture of the people and the district of Saint Antine. The signs of hunger and sickness are everywhere. Young children have old faces and grave voices. In the bakeries are a few small loaves of bad bread; in the sausage shop are dog-meat sausages and there are few of these to be seen; in the wine-shops thin wine and beer are served; and everywhere are the faces with hunted looks, with desperation in the eyes, as of some wild beast at bay who turns upon its attackers.

The wine-shop keeper, Monsieur Defarge, has been observing all the activity in front of his shop, and when he sees the citizen Gaspard write "blood" on the wall, he admonishes him, picks up a handful of mud, obliterates the word and re-enters his shop.

COMMENT: Monsieur Defarge, who is to play such a major part in future events, is not pleased with Gaspard's joke. It is too soon, the time is not yet. The conspiracy of silence must remain such for some years to come.

Defarge is described as "a bull-necked, martial-looking man of thirty . . . good-humored looking on the whole, but implacable-looking, too; a man of strong resolution and a set purpose." Madame Defarge, who is sitting behind the counter of the wine-shop as her husband enters, is an ideal match for her husband, with her "strong features, composure of manner" and "watchful eye that seldom seemed to look at anything." She is sitting with her knitting before her, and with a raise of her eyebrow she informs her husband that he should look round the shop at the customers to note any new arrivals.

COMMENT: Madame Defarge will be shown to be even stronger and more implacable than her husband when the Revolution is under way. The knitting which she is never without will serve the revolutionaries well in the future uprising.

Monsieur Defarge surveys the customers, pretends not to notice the elderly gentleman and the young lady at one of the tables, and proceeds to the counter where he falls into conversation with three men standing there. The discussion centers around the wine incident and the fact that it is not often that these miserable people know the taste of wine. "So much the worse," comments one of the three. "A bitter taste it is that such poor cattle always have in their mouths, and hard lives they live, Jacques. Am I not right, Jacques?" "You are right, Jacques," is the reply of Monsieur Defarge.

COMMENT: During this conversation, the three men and Monsieur Defarge address each other as "Jacques" which identifies them as fellow conspirators in the peasant uprising to come. The name comes from "Jacques Bonhomme" (Goodman James), a term contemptuously applied by the nobles to the peasantry who revolted in 1358 against their oppressors. Thus, "Jacquerie" is the term applied to any revolt of French peasants.

Monsieur Defarge informs the three men of the location of a furnished lodging that they have expressed an interest in and they pay for their wine and leave the shop. Thereupon the elderly gentleman, Mr. Lorry, leaves his table and whispers a few words to Defarge. Defarge nods and goes out. Mr. Lorry signals to his companion, Lucie Manette, and they, too, go out and meet Defarge in a courtyard nearby. During all this, Madame Defarge has sat, knitting, seemingly noticing nothing but, in reality, seeing everything. Defarge's face has changed. The good humor is gone and there is no openness about him. Instead, he has now the look of a "secret, angry, dangerous man." Defarge leads Mr. Lorry and Miss Manette up a long staircase in a building nearby. The decayed refuse on the stair of this ramshackle building poisons the air and increases the agitation that both Mr. Lorry and Miss Manette feel. "Is he alone?" asks Mr. Lorry. "Alone! God help him, who should be with him?" answers Defarge in a low voice. "Is he always alone, then?" "Yes." "He is greatly changed?" "Changed!" Defarge answers, and mutters a tremendous curse and strikes the wall with his hand.

At last they reach the garret where Dr. Manette is hidden away and Defarge pauses to take out a key from his coat. Mr. Lorry asks why it is necessary to keep him locked in and Defarge's answer is "Why! Because he has lived so long, locked up, that he would be frightened — rave — tear himself to pieces — die — come to I know not what harm — if his door was left open." Although these words do not recah Lucie's ears, she is by this time trembling with anxiety and terror at the prospect which awaits her. As they enter the room of the garret, they see the three men named Jacques who left the wine-shop just before them. Defarge sends them away and Mr. Lorry, a bit angry, inquires whether Dr. Manette is put on show? To which Monsieur Defarge replies that he does show Dr. Manette to certain men, "to whom the sight is likely to do good." Defarge bangs loudly on a door to an adjoining room, to prepare the gentleman within for a visit, then he opens it, admits himself, Mr. Lorry, and Miss Manette, and locks the door behind them. The room is dim and dark but as the three stand by the door and their eyes grow accustomed to the darkness they see a white-haired man, sitting on a low bench, making shoes.

> **COMMENT:** Here we first meet Dr. Manette for whom Lucie and Mr. Lorry have made their difficult trip. He has been released, for unknown reasons, after many years in prison and has been put in the care of Monsieur Defarge, who is a former servant of the Manette family. His imprisonment has befogged Dr. Manette's mind, and all he knows of himself is that he is a shoemaker, a trade which he taught himself in prison. Defarge uses the sight of Dr. Manette in this pitiful condition to enflame the hearts of his fellow conspirators and to keep the fire of revolution burning until the time is ripe for action.

CHAPTER 6. THE SHOEMAKER

Defarge greets the shoemaker and in a very faint voice Dr. Manette responds: "Good day!" "You are still hard at work, I see?" "Yes — I am working." The replies come only after a long silence as if it were difficult for the old man to form the words. The shoemaker's voice is faint, a mere echo of a voice, a voice which has lost its tone and color through years of solitude and disuse. Defarge speaks again: "I want to let in a little more light here. You can bear a little more?" "I must bear it, if you let it in," the small voice replies. The extra light reveals Dr. Manette more clearly to his visitors. He has a hollow, thin face with a raggedly-cut white beard and white hair, and large, bright eyes. His tattered clothes reveal the thin, withered body beneath them.

Dr. Manette resumes work on the shoes as Defarge motions to Mr. Lorry to come closer. "You have a visitor," says Defarge, "who knows a well-made shoe when he sees one. Tell Monsieur what kind of shoe it is, and the maker's name." After the question is repeated the answer comes: "It is a lady's shoe." "And the maker's name?" "Did you ask me for my name?" "Assuredly, I did." "One Hundred and Five, North Tower." "You are not a shoemaker by trade?" asks Mr. Lorry. After a pause, "No, I was not a shoemaker by trade. I learnt it here. I taught myself. I asked leave to." "Monsieur Manette, do you remember nothing of me? Is there no old banker, no old business, no old servant, no old time, rising in your mind, Monsieur Manette?" Dr. Manette looks fixedly, first at Mr. Lorry then at Monsieur Defarge, and for a moment the mist seems to clear from his eyes, but then they are clouded over again. The expression is repeated on Lucie's face. She has been standing nearby trembling with eagerness to love the spectral face of her father back to life and hope. Lucie approaches and stands near the bench. At first the old man does not notice her but is engrossed in his work. Then he spies her dress and looks up at her, fear in his eyes. "What is this?" With tears streaming down her cheeks Lucie kisses her father's hands and embraces him. He recoils at first but the sight of her golden hair awakens a distant memory in his mind and he touches it. Then he puts his hand to his neck and takes a folded rag from a string and opens it. Inside, there are two or three golden hairs which he holds in his fingers and compares to Lucie's hair. It is the same! He recalls the night that he was taken to the prison. He found these strands of hair on his shoulder, left there when his daughter embraced him as he left the house. "How was this? Was it you?" The old man is amazed at this new, strange event and for a moment he tears at his hair in a frenzy. He cannot believe that this young, beautiful girl is the daughter he was torn from so many years ago. But he becomes calm again and his softened tone causes his daughter to kneel before him and embrace him. At the same time she asks for his blessing and vows that she will nurse him back to health and devote her life to this man whose fate she had been unaware of, to return with him to England to be at peace and at rest. Lucie is transported with both sadness and joy. "Good gentlemen, thank you! I feel his sacred tears upon my face, and his sobs strike against my heart. O, see! Thank God for us, thank God!"

This great storm of emotion which has taken place in both of them is finally past and the old man lies nestled in the arms of his loving daughter. Lucie asks Mr. Lorry if he will make arrangements for them to leave Paris at once. Mr. Lorry doubts that the doctor is well enough to travel, but Lucie feels that the most important thing is for Dr. Manette to leave France and Defarge agrees. Lucie asks the two men to leave her alone with her father, and although thy are disinclined to do so, Lucie prevails and the two men hurry out to make arrangements for the trip back to England. Soon all is in readiness, and they return to the garret with food and clothing for Dr. Manette. The events of the day have confused him and his bewilderment and occasional frenzied clasping of his head with his hands frighten his friends and they agree to ask no further questions for the moment. Mr. Manette takes the food they offer him and puts on the clothing in a submissive way, in the way of a man long accustomed to obeying orders. During all of this, Lucie is at his side and he finds pleasure and strength in her voice and her touch.

As they board the coach that is to take them back to England, Doctor Manette plaintively asks for his shoemaking tools and the unfinished shoes. Madame Defarge, who has been standing nearby in the courtyard, knitting, calls that she will get them. She hands them into the coach and resumes her position leaning against a post — knitting and seeing nothing. Defarge gives the command to the postilion (the coachman) — "To the barrier!" and the coach clatters away. When they reach the guard house, a soldier asks for their papers. Defarge gets down from the coach, gives Dr. Manette's papers to the guard, whispers a few words to him and the guard holds a lantern into the coach, saying, "It is well. Forward." Defarge bids adieu to the travelers, and the coach goes on its way. All through the night's ride, Mr. Jarvis Lorry, sitting opposite Dr. Manette and wondering about him, thinks of the old inquiry: "I hope you are to be recalled to life?" "I can't say."

COMMENT: With this chapter, Book One of "A Tale of Two Cities" comes to a close. We have met several of the important characters who are to figure in the later action of the story and we have learned of the return to life of Dr. Manette, so long imprisoned and so miserably changed through the ordeal. Mr. Lorry, the Defarges, and Lucie Manette once again find their lives intertwined with that of Dr. Manette. Many more people are to be drawn into this circle of influence and find themselves caught up in the events which will come to pass because of that dark night, eighteen years ago, when Dr. Alexandre Manette, physician, was taken from his home and transformed into "One Hundred and Five, North Tower."

BOOK THE SECOND — THE GOLDEN THREAD

CHAPTER 1.   FIVE YEARS LATER

The first chapter of Book Two opens in London with a description of that venerable institution represented by Mr. Jarvis Lorry — Tellson's Bank. Tellson's is an old firm and things have not changed there very much since its founding. The building in which it is housed is small, dark and ugly. A customer, in order to do business with Tellson's, must fight his way through an obstinate door, trip down two steps, and find himself before a small counter presided over by an ancient clerk whose hands shake as he holds a check up to the meager light entering through a mud-splattered window to verify a signature. But any suggestion that Tellson's be spruced up a bit and made more cheery and comfortable for customers would be received as heresy, and anyone making such a suggestion would be shown the door. For Tellson's has always been thus and will remain so, for the belief is strong that this is what makes Tellson's a respectable firm and changing it would somehow make it no longer respectable. The same is true of the personnel. Dickens writes: "When they took a young man into Tellson's London house, they hid him somewhere till he was old. They kept him in a dark place, like a cheese, until he had full Tellson flavor and blue-mould upon him. Then only was he permitted to be seen, spectacularly poring over large books, and casting his breeches and gaiters into the general weight of the establishment."

Outside Tellson's is usually to be seen the odd-job man Jerry Cruncher, whom we have met earlier. During business hours Jerry sits waiting outside the bank for any errand that needs to be run, and when he is out on an errand, his twelve-year-old son, who is the very image of his father, waits in his place.

The scene is Jerry Cruncher's lodgings: a small, two-room apartment in an unsavory neighborhood. The place, however, is kept neat and clean by Mrs. Cruncher. It is 7:30 A.M. and Jerry is beginning to stir from slumber, his spiky hair threatening to tear the sheets to ribbons. The first words from his mouth as he awakes are "Bust me, if she ain't at it again!" An orderly-looking woman who has been on her knees in the corner of the room leaps to her feet with haste at Jerry's words. In his annoyance at his wife, Jerry throws one of his muddy boots at her. The fact that there is often mud on Jerry's boots in the morning is unusual, for when he returns home from his day's work at the bank his boots are usually clean.

Mrs. Cruncher protests that she was only saying her prayers, but the statement only irritates Jerry more, for he takes particular exception to her saying her prayers for some reason. "What do you mean by flopping yourself down and praying agin me?" "I was not praying against you; I was praying for you," replies Mrs. Cruncher. "You weren't. And if you were, I won't be took the liberty with." Jerry is in a foul mood and remains so through breakfast, accusing his wife of taking the bread from her son's mouth through her "praying against" Jerry. It seems that Jerry's night trade, that mysterious occupation that muddies his boots, has not been going well and there has been no money coming from it. It is clear to Jerry that this state of affairs can be directly attributed to Mrs. Cruncher and her "flopping." For Mrs. Cruncher is not happy with Jerry's second occupation and offers up her prayers that he might see the error of his ways and give it up. And Jerry continues to upbraid his wife right up until the time that he and young Jerry leave for Tellson's Bank, where they take up their positions on a stool outside. Shortly after their arrival, Jerry is called inside, for a messenger is wanted. Young Jerry takes his father's place on the stool and mutters to himself. "Always rusty! His fingers is always rusty! Where does my father get all that iron rust from? He don't get no iron rust here!"

> **COMMENT:** Another mention of Jerry's second occupation. It is as much a mystery to young Jerry as it is to us at the moment. We only know that it worries Mrs. Cruncher and that Jerry has not had much luck at it lately. In a short while we, and young Jerry, will follow Jerry Cruncher on one of his night excursions, one which will not only clear up the mystery for us but which will provide a needed trump card in a difficult situation much later in the book.

CHAPTER 2.   A SIGHT

Jerry learns that his errand is to go to the Old Bailey, England's famous Criminal Courts Building, make his presence known to Mr. Lorry who is there, and wait, in case the old gentleman should have need of him. The case being tried on this particular morning involves a charge of treason, a charge for which a man adjudged guilty is given the punishment of quartering.

> **COMMENT:** The penalties throughout the world in those days, and in some places to this day, were quite severe even for minor offenses such as stealing a loaf of bread. For such a theft, a man might lose a limb or even his life. The high crime of treason carried this horrible punishment: the man would be half hanged, then he would be disemboweled while still alive, and then decap-

itated and his body cut into quarters. A not uncommon punishment in England or France in the 18th Century.

Jerry finds the custom of quartering barbarous and says so to the old bank clerk who tells him his errand. The man is shocked by Jerry's statement. "It is the law," he says to Jerry, as if this made everything all right.

Jerry proceeds to the court, makes his presence known to Mr. Lorry, and settles back in the crowded courtroom to await developments. Seated at the table with Mr. Lorry are two bewigged gentlemen — one the prisoners counsel, surrounded by papers concerning the case, and near him another man whose whole attention, now and during the course of the trial, seems to be concentrated on the ceiling of the court. As the prisoner is brought in, all eyes are riveted on him — a young, handsome man, about twenty-five, obviously a gentleman. The great interest that the crowd shows in this young man is directly attributable to the dire punishment which will be meted out to him — the word "will" is placed there because there is no doubt in their minds that such punishment will indeed be forthcoming. One can feel the excitement that the crowd is experiencing at the prospect of blood.

The indictment is read. The prisoner, one Charles Darnay, has been charged with spying for the French king against the Crown of England to provide details about the forces being prepared to be sent to North America. To this charge the prisoner has pleaded not guilty. The prisoner, as he listens to the charges being read to the court, appears outwardly calm, though somewhat pale beneath his dark complexion, and his wandering eyes come to rest on two persons seated near the Judge's bench. His attention becomes immediately affixed on these two, so much so that the eyes of the crowd follow his glance. The two who receive so much attention are an intense man with white hair whose expression makes him at one moment seem old and at another seem in the prime of his life; and with him a young lady, obviously his daughter. Her face is lit with terror and compassion for the accused. A buzzing runs through the crowd, each one wondering who these two are and the word finally reaches Jerry as to their identity. "Witnesses." "For which side?" "Against." "Against which side?" "The prisoner's." And the Attorney-General rises to verbally hang, disembowel, and quarter the accused.

COMMENT: We catch our first glimpses of three more characters in this story: Charles Darnay, the accused; Mr. Stryver, his defense counsel (whose first name we never learn); and Sydney Carton, Mr. Stryver's associate, the man whose attention seems to be directed to the ceiling during the court proceedings. These three, in their turn, are drawn into the circle of influence of Dr. Manette and Lucie, and in being so drawn are to experience, among them, joy, disappointment, terror, and death. It soon becomes clear that Mr. Sydney Carton's attention has not wandered as far as we were given to think, for his observation of the prisoner is to give the defense counsel a strong weapon in achieving acquittal of Charles Darnay and this same weapon will be used once again to save Darnay's life in France later.

CHAPTER 3. A DISAPPOINTMENT

The Attorney-General's approach is a melodramatic one, designed to make the jury and the crowd feel hatred and resentment toward the accused and pride and favor toward the prosecution's chief witness, one John Barsad. According to the Attorney-General, Barsad is a noble soul who, though a friend of the accused until he learned of his nefarious undertakings, then felt obliged to turn him in for the good of the country, he being a true patriot, a great public benefactor, and an unimpeachable witness for the Crown. And the jury, being a loyal jury and a responsible jury, "must positively find the prisoner Guilty, and make an end of him, whether they liked it or not." This opening speech does not fail to stir the hearts of the jury and the crowd against the prisoner and the room buzzes over the Attorney-General's speech.

The Solicitor-General's questioning of the witness underlines all the sterling qualities of Mr. Barsad which had already been enumerated by the Attorney-General and it is then the Defense Counsel's turn. Mr. Stryver's questioning of the witness paints Mr. Barsad a good deal more black than white. The testimony brings out the fact that Mr. Barsad lives upon his property but he doesn't remember at the moment where said property is; that he has been in debtor's prison a number of times; that he has borrowed money from the prisoner and has not repaid it. The Crown's second witness, Roger Cly, who was engaged as a servant by the accused, gives testimony to the effect that he became suspicious of Darnay and kept an eye on him. He often noticed Darnay with mysterious lists and saw him show these lists to French gentlemen at Calais and Boulogne. In the course of his testimony, Cly, too, is shown to have an unsavory past and a long acquaintance with Barsad. Cly also claims that he is testifying through motives of sheer patriotism. But the seed has been planted by Stryver that suggests that neither Barsad nor Cly is to be trusted, that they are probably paid informers in the service of the Crown.

Mr. Jarvis Lorry is then called to the stand. The prosecutor attempts to persuade Mr. Lorry that Charles Darnay was one of the passengers with him in the coach from London to Dover but Mr. Lorry cannot identify him. He has, however, seen the accused before, when they both were on the same packet boat making the return trip from Calais to Dover, across the Channel. The fact that Darnay boarded the ship alone in the dead of night is given an unsavory connotation. Then Lucie Manette is called. Her earnestness, her youth and beauty, and her pity are too much for Charles Darnay and he is shaken as he stands in the prisoner's dock. Miss Manette and her father were with Mr. Lorry on the trip referred to above and she spoke with the prisoner on that occasion. Lucie is very hesitant about giving her testimony, for she does not wish to repay his kindness on that occasion by doing him harm today. She testifies that Darnay told her then that he was traveling under an assumed name on business of a delicate nature and his business might require frequent trips between France and England. She also mentions that he conferred with two French gentlemen up until the moment when the boat sailed for England. He also mentioned to her that in the quarrel between England and the American colonies that England was wrong and foolish, and added, in a jesting way, that "perhaps George Washington might gain almost as great a name in history as George the Third," a statement which does not go down well with the court. Dr. Manette is also called as a witness, but he can offer no information, for he has no recollection of what occurred on that Channel voyage five years ago.

The next witness is called on to testify that he saw the accused at a certain hotel in a garrison-town waiting for another person. The witness is quite sure that it was the prisoner that he saw on that occasion. At this point, Mr. Stryver's associate, Sydney Carton, the gentleman who has been staring at the ceiling, tosses a note to Stryver who, upon reading it, looks with great atteention and curiosity at the prisoner. Stryver asks the witness again if he is sure in his identification. The witness says yes. "Look well upon that gentleman, my learned friend there," says Stryver, pointing to him who had passed the paper over, "and then look well upon the prisoner. How say you? Are they very like each other?" Despite the fact that the appearance of Mr. Carton is slovenly, not to say debauched, the resemblance is astounding and is made even more so when Carton removes his wig. The result of this dramatic encounter is to destroy the witness' testimony utterly.

Stryver then sums up his case: Barsad and Cly are villains, in cahoots with each other and with the Government; the trips Darnay makes between France and England are indeed business affairs; and, in short, the evidence is very meager and circumstantial. Following which the Attorney-General makes his summation and the Judge makes his charge to the Jury. The Jury then turns to consider a verdict. At this point Sydney

Carton notices that Lucie Manette has fainted upon her father's breast and calls out, "Officer! Look to that young lady. Help the gentleman to take her out. Don't you see she will fall!" Lucie is led out by her father whose face shows that old brooding, pondering look which came upon him while he was offering testimony and had remained there during the trial.

The jury, after some discussion, announces that they cannot agree and wish to retire for further discussion. The trial has gone on all day and the lamps in the court are now being lighted. The crowd withdraws for refreshment and Mr. Lorry gives Jerry Cruncher permission to do the same but charges him to be back when the verdict is announced so that he may take it back to Tellson's. Carton goes to Darnay and calms his fears concerning Lucie Manette and promises to convey Darnay's message of regret for having caused her such distress.

An hour and a half later, with a rapid tide of people pouring up the stairs to the courtroom, Mr. Lorry appears at the door calling for Jerry. That worthy messenger appears and reaches through the throng to accept a paper from Lorry's fingers. On it is written one word: "Acquitted."

> **COMMENT:** Charles Darnay has been acquitted to live through a far greater ordeal in the future. Acquitted, through the intercession of Mr. Sydney Carton, a slovenly, debauched associate of Stryver's who has seemed to be unconcerned with all that was going on about him during the trial and who does not seem to be greatly concerned with Charles Darnay, even though he helped to save him. But this strange, enigmatic man was the first to notice Lucie's distress and to call for aid. This admiration and concern for Lucie Manette will cause him once again to shake off his carelessness and disinterest to preserve her happiness. He will be aided in this later action by Mr. Barsad who will turn up again in a different role.

CHAPTER 4. CONGRATULATORY

As the last remnants of spectators are leaving the courtroom, several principals in this drama — the Manettes, Mr. Lorry, and Mr. Stryver — are found gathered around Charles Darnay, congratulating him on his recent escape from death. Dr. Manette is quite changed from the man we met in Paris. He is alert, intelligent, upright and bearing. Only when that cloud passes over his face, as it still does from time to time, does he revert to his old appearance. But Lucie's loving care has restored him to his former self, and her voice and the touch of her hand banish the cloud when it appears. Charles Darnay kisses Lucie's hand in gratitude and warmly thanks Mr. Stryver for his defense. Mr. Stryver, a man of about thirty who looks twenty years older, "stout, loud, red, bluff, and free from any drawback of delicacy," is enjoying his success, for it clearly will help him in furthering his ambitions. During the exchange of courtesies Dr. Manette has been silent, staring at Charles Darnay intently, with a look of dislike, distrust and fear.

> **COMMENT:** There is something in Charles Darnay's face which awakens a spark of recognition in Dr. Manette's mind. He cannot quite place it, but there is something about it which disturbs him and which, when he learns the truth of it on Lucie's wedding day, will cause the cloud to fall over his face more completely and disastrously than it has since that day five years ago when he was recalled to life.

Mr. Lorry calls attention to Dr. Manette's look and Lucie hurries him off in a coach. Mr. Stryver withdraws, leaving Mr. Lorry and Charles Darnay together. At this point Sydney Carton, who has been standing in the shadows, joins them. No one has made any mention of Carton's part in the acquittal, for only Stryver and Darnay know of it. "So. Mr. Lorry! Men of business may speak to Mr. Darnay now?" says Carton sarcastically, referring to Mr. Lorry's hesitation in speaking with Darnay in the courtroom because of his connection with Tellson's. Mr. Lorry is nettled by the sarcasm and by the appearance of this careless, haphazard man who seems to care for nothing, and he answers sharply: "We men of business are not our own masters. And indeed, sir, I really don't know what you have to do with the matter . . . I really don't know that it is your business." "Business! Bless you, *I* have no business," answers Mr. Carton. "It is a pity you have not, sir. If you had perhaps you would attend to it." "Lord love you, no! I shouldn't." Thoroughly angered by the man's indifference, Mr. Lorry bids goodby to Charles Darnay and departs.

Carton takes Darnay to a nearby tavern where Darnay sits down to a meal after his ordeal while Carton sits opposite him with a bottle of port. As they sit together, Carton, in his half-insolent manner, baits Darnay. "That's a fair young lady to be pitied by and wept for by! How does it feel? Is it worth being tried for one's life, to be the object of such sympathy and compassion, Mr. Darnay?" Darnay does not reply to the question but instead thanks Carton for his help in the trial. Carton rejects this — "I neither want any thanks, nor merit any. Mr. Darnay, let me ask you a question. Do you think I particularly like you?" "You have acted as if you do; but I don't think you do." "I don't think I do," agrees Carton, whereupon Darnay expresses a wish to part friends, pays the bill and rises to leave. Then, all of Carton's bitterness comes to the surface. "I am a disappointed drudge, sir, I care for no man on earth, and no man on earth cares for me." As Darnay leaves, Carton considers his image in a mirror. Why should he like a man who resembles himself? For he only reminds him of what he, Carton, might have been. And then to have those blue eyes and fair face show pity and despair for Darnay. "Come on, and have it out in plain words! You hate the fellow." And with his pint of wine for consolation, Carton falls asleep with his head resting on the table.

> **COMMENT:** The enigmatic Sydney Carton confronts his look-alike at close range and makes it clear to Charles Darnay that he cares not a jot for him. But the figure of Lucie Manette looms up before the two men and it is clear that she has the same effect on both of these men who look so much alike but are so different. It is in her reflected light that each would like to bask, but Carton knows that for him it is impossible and so he hates the man for whom it *is possible* and who, if things had been different, he might have been.

CHAPTER 5. THE JACKAL

In eighteenth-century England men were hard drinkers and Mr. Stryver and Sydney Carton are no exceptions; on many a night the two men drink together to the wee hours of the morning. Mr. Stryver has become a favorite at the Old Bailey and his foot is on the lower rungs of the ladder of success. In the early days of his career it was noted that although Mr. Stryver was a bold, glib, unscrupulous man (all of which characteristics pointed to success), he had not the ability of extracting from a mass of documents relating to a case the salient points, the essence. But since his acquaintance with Sydney Carton a remarkable improvement was noticed in this score, and whatever the case being tried in which Stryver was involved, Carton would be seated nearby staring at the ceiling.

Thus, at ten P.M., when Sydney Carton is awakened by a servant after having fallen asleep over his wine, he proceeds to Mr. Stryver's lodgings where the two begin work on the documents for the next day's cases. After preparing himself with a supply of towels and a jug of cold water, Sydney Carton attacks the two piles of papers provided by Mr. Stryver. The two men partake frequently of the punch on a nearby table and Sydney, when in the midst of a knotty problem, arises to change the damp towel on his forehead.

At long last Sydney has extracted the essence of the documents and Stryver has made his selections and composed his remarks on them, and at three A.M. the two men refill their glasses and sit to chat. Carton's replies are somewhat short but Stryver is used to the vagaries of his colleague. "The old seesaw Sydney. Up one minute and down the next." Stryver then assumes a pompous manner and begins to lecture Carton. "Carton, your way is, and always was, a lame way. You summon no energy and purpose. Look at me." But Sydney refuses to be baited and with a laugh replies, "Oh, botheration! Don't *you* be moral!" We learn from the conversation that the two men were classmates at Shrewsbury School and even then Sydney Carton did others' work for them while neglecting his own; and even then Stryver was shouldering himself ahead while Carton was left behind. Sydney wearies of the talk and rises to leave, at which point Stryver comments on the "pretty witness" at the court today. Carton immediately bridles at this insufficient description of Lucie Manette. *"She* pretty? She was a golden-haired doll!" Stryver picks up this passionate outburst of Carton's and comments that Sydney seemed very aware of Lucie at the trial. Carton makes light of his host's remark and bids him good night

As Sydney Carton makes his way home the air is cold, the sky overcast. In this bleak atmosphere the image of Lucie Manette, which has been called to mind, causes Carton to see before him "a mirage of honorable ambitions, self-denial and perserverance," but only for a moment. As he sadly reaches his lodgings and throws himself fully clothed onto his bed, the sun rises, rises on this man of good talents and emotions, who somehow is unable to shake off the sickness of spirit that is eating him away and who resigns himself to the bleakness of the life that he lives.

COMMENT: Stryver and Carton are an unlikely combination at first sight. But these two who have known each other since school days have built a relationship which contributes mightily to Stryver's success as a lawyer. Sydney Carton's quickness and penetrating mind are just what Stryver needs, and the relationship of "lion" and "jackal" results in Stryver's being well thought of in the law courts and provides Carton with the few necessities of life he requires, although his talents remain unappreciated by all except Stryver. And though Carton can see that his present life is a waste, that his talents might be put to better use than serving as mental drudge to a pompous, successful lawyer, he is unable to change his situation. In the holocaust to come he will attain his true stature and win a place of respect in the hearts of those who now think him mean and despicable.

CHAPTER 6. HUNDREDS OF PEOPLE

It is Mr. Jarvis Lorry's custom to spend Sunday afternoons with the Manettes in their quiet lodging near Soho Square in London. It is now four months since the treason trial and the memory of it is gone from the public's mind. Doctor Manette and Lucie occupy two floors of a house which is otherwise occupied by a few quiet artisans who are little seen or heard. The doctor has established a small practice here which provides him and Lucie with as much money as they need to live. Lucie and Doctor Manette are not at home when Mr. Lorry arrives, but since he is quite at home here, he enters the house and walks through the rooms. In the doctor's bedroom, in a corner, he sees the disused shoemaker's bench and tools. "I wonder that he keeps that reminder of his sufferings about him!" Mr. Lorry says softly. "And why wonder at that," comes the reply, so unexpectedly as to make Mr. Lorry start. It is spoken by Miss Pross who, as she served Lucie for so many years, now serves Lucie and her father. Miss Pross assumes a proprietary air over Lucie, and she resents the "dozens of people" who come to the house looking after her "Ladybird" (Lucie). *"Do* dozens come for that purpose?" asks Mr. Lorry. "Hundreds," replies Miss Pross. In Miss Pross' mind even Dr. Manette is not worthy of such a daughter, but she could have accepted him if there hadn't been dozens of others to take Ladybird's affection away from her. As a matter of fact there is only one man on the face of this earth who is, in the opinion of Miss Pross, worthy of Lucie and that is Miss Pross' brother, Solomon. Despite the fact that Solomon coldly took all her money and possessions and left her behind in poverty, deserting her without compunction, she still believes in his basic worth. This belief remains unshakeable.

> COMMENT: We have already met Solomon under another name and we, and Miss Pross, are to see him again in Paris where Sydney Carton obtains his grudging assistance in a daring scheme.

Mr. Lorry and Miss Pross discuss the presence of the shoemaking equipment and find it remarkable that Dr. Manette has never broached the subject of his imprisonment to anyone, not even Lucie, in the years since his release. Miss Pross comments that the subject is a painful one for the Doctor and whenever it is approached he instantly changes for the worse. Often in the night Doctor Manette can be heard walking to and fro in his room, tormented by something from the past. On these occasions Lucie goes to him and walks with him until he is composed, but never does he say anything about the reason for his restlessness and Lucie has found it wiser not to hint at it to him. Lucie and Dr. Manette return home from their walk and Miss Pross busies herself over Lucie, taking her bonnet and folding her mantle.

Dinner time arrives and still no hundreds of people. Only Lucie and Dr. Manette, Mr. Lorry and Miss Pross. After dinner, as they are sipping their wine in the garden, Charles Darnay arrives. In the conversation Darnay tells a curious story he heard while he was imprisoned in the Tower of London before his trial. It seems that an old dungeon which had been covered over for some years was discovered and on one of the corner stones was written the word "Dig." The workmen dug beneath the stone and found a leather bag inside of which were fragments of paper, which had deteriorated so that whatever had been written could never be read. At the conclusion of this story Dr. Manette starts and puts his hands to his head. Lucie is frightened by his look but he recovers himself almost immediately and calmly says that he started because of some drops of rain that had struck him. It is indeed beginning to rain and the friends go inside where they are joined at ten by Sydney Carton, and they all sit and look out the window as the storm gathers momentum. Lucie remarks that sometimes, when she has sat before this same window of an evening, she has thought that the echoes of the footsteps in the streets before the house are the footsteps of people who are coming, by-and-by, into their lives. Indeed, many footsteps can be heard rushing and echoing through the storm and the sounds of lightning and thunder and torrents of rain underline this picture of multitudes rushing down upon them.

COMMENT: Charles Darnay's story has brought a shock of recognition to Dr. Manette. For as he looks at Darnay with that same look of dislike and fear which we noted at the trial he recalls that he, too, has written something during his imprisonment and buried it in his cell. That document is one day to be discovered, intact, and is to cause much anguish and pain to him and to Lucie as well, and will cause Charles Darnay to once again go on trial for his life. The great crowd of people that Lucie senses will soon enter their lives is already forming and will sweep into their lives in a very short while, bringing death and destruction.

CHAPTER 7.   MONSEIGNEUR IN TOWN

The Monseigneur of the chapter's title is one of the great lords of the court. This great lord takes his pleasure at the opera and at private suppers at his estate where it takes four men, besides the cook, to present his chocolate to him. To Monseigneur the world was made for his pleasures and France exists to fill his pocket; there is no doubt in his mind that this will be the order of things unendingly. In this unreal world exist military men with no military knowledge; naval officers with no idea of a ship; civil officers without a notion of civil affairs. And not far from this palatial mansion, the scene of great suppers and balls attended by gallant gentlemen and fine ladies and catered to by multitudes of servants, is the town full of peasants, scarecrows dressed in rags. And the rustle of fine silks and brocades fans the devouring hunger of the multitudes of the downtrodden citizenry.

> **COMMENT:** The ironic tone that Dickens used in the opening chapter is used once again here with devastating effect. The air of unreality, as of wooden puppets performing in a highly stylized court drama pervades the description. The reality of hunger and oppression will, before long, topple the walls of this little theater and break the puppets to bits.

As the grand evening comes to an end and the Monseigneur retires, his guests prepare to levae. One gentleman, who has stood a little apart during the evening and has been treated coldly by the Monseigneur, leaves in anger. This gentleman, a Marquis, is about sixty, haughty in manner with a transparently handsome face that has a suggestion of cruelty in it. The Marquis enters his carriage and is driven at breakneck speed through the town.

Turning the corner, there is a jolt, a loud cry, and the horses rear up and plunge. The Marquis, calmly looking out, says, "What has gone wrong?" A child has been run down and a man is weeping over it in the street. It is the father of the child and he is moaning piteously over his own. The people stand around looking cowed — they have been downtrodden so long that there is no hint of rage or hatred in their faces. The Marquis is annoyed at this inconvenience. He takes out his purse. "It is extraordinary to me that you people cannot take care of yourselves and your children. One or the other of you is forever in the way. How do I know what injury you have done my horses? See! Give him that," and he tosses a coin to the ground. Another man appears on the scene and comforts the weeping father. "Be a brave man, Gaspard. It is better for the poor little plaything to die so, than to live." This new arrival is Defarge, keeper of the wine-shop, and his remarks please the Marquis, who throws him another coin and begins to drive away. Suddenly, the coin is flung back into the coach. The enraged Marquis stops the coach and looks out but Defarge is nowhere to be seen, and in his anger the Marquis does not notice the woman standing nearby staring at him, and knitting. As the coach and its retinue depart, she remains there and knits on with the steadfastness of fate.

> **COMMENT:** Peasant life is cheap to the nobility of France. A child is killed under the horses' hooves, a coin is thrown out, and

it is all forgotten by the Marquis who is able to pay for anything he breaks. But it is not forgotten by the father of the child — Gaspard, the man who wrote the word "blood" on a wall with a wine-soaked hand and whose prophetic word has struck at his own being and which word will become even more prophetic when the hand which was once soaked with wine is soaked with blood. And it is not forgotten by Madame Defarge who sees all. Like the three fates of Greek mythology, she, with her knitting, is recording the life span of many Frenchmen and those who earn her attention will find their lives shortened considerably.

CHAPTER 8. MONSEIGNEUR IN THE COUNTRY

The Marquis is riding in his carriage through the broken landscape. He passes through a village — a typical village with its poor streets, its poor tavern, and its poor people. The cause of their poverty is clear, for everywhere there are indications as to where all the many taxes are to be paid in the village. The coach pulls up at the posting-house gate, having been preceded by a courier. The people in the vicinity stop what they are doing to look at the Marquis and he casts his eye an the submissive faces before him. One catches his eye. "Bring me hither that fellow!" he commands. The man is brought before him and questioned. The carriage passed the man on the road and the Marquis noticed that he stared fixedly as it went by. At what? "Monseigneur, I looked at the man. He swung by the chain of the shoe." The man cannot identify this man who rode beneath the carriage and the Marquis is exasperated by him. "Did the man run away, Dolt?" "Monseigneur, he precipitated himself over the hill-side, head first, as a person plunges into the river." The Marquis instructs Gabelle, the local functionary, to be on the watch for this mysterious rider and he drives away.

As the carriage reaches the top of a hill a woman rushes up to beg a petition. With impatience the Marquis hears her out. Her husband, the forester, has died and she asks only that a piece of stone or wood, with his name upon it, be placed over him to show where he lies. For there are many buried under poor heaps of grass and the place will be quickly forgotten when she dies. The valet pushes her away from the door and the carriage proceeds on to the Marquis' chateau. As he steps from the coach to the door of the chateau he asks a servant, "Monsieur Charles, whom I expect; is he arrived from England?" "Monseigneur, not yet."

COMMENT: Another description of the abject misery in which the French people live and the callousness of the nobility toward their suffering. But a new bit of news has stirred up the villagers

— a mender of roads has seen an unidentified man hanging from the underside of the Marquis' carriage. This extraordinary event occupies their full attention. What can it mean? If the Marquis is preoccupied with its meaning as he leaves the village, we do not learn of it. But he soon will have an explanation for it — the man beneath the carriage, covered with dust and looking like a specter, is Gaspard, whose child has recently been killed beneath the wheels of the Marquis' carriage.

CHAPTER 9.   THE GORGON'S HEAD

The Marquis' chateau is a massive building, all of stone—stone flowers, stone urns, and stone faces of men decorate its facade as if the Gorgon, who, in ancient mythology turned men to stone with a glance, had cast her eye upon the chateau two centuries ago.

The Marquis proceeds up the stone staircase, preceded by a torch bearer. The night is black and there is no sound to be heard save the hoot of an owl disturbed by the light. The Marquis reaches his private apartment upstairs. The rooms are sumptuously decorated as befits such a nobleman and a supper-table for two has been laid in one of the rooms. The Marquis prepares himself and in a quarter of an hour sits down to his choice supper. As he dines he thinks he notices a shadow at the window, but a servant investigates and there is nothing to be seen but the black night outside. When he is about half-way through his meal, the sound of a carriage is heard. It is the nephew of the Marquis who has been expected. We have met this nephew before: it is Charles Darnay.

The servant withdraws and the two men converse during their supper. It is clear that there exists deep distrust and enmity between uncle and nephew. Indeed, it is clear that the uncle would be content to have Charles out of the way, for it is suggested that the trial of treason was somehow connected with his uncle's efforts. "I believe that if you were not in disgrace with the Court, a letter *de cachet* would have sent me to some fortress indefinitely," says Charles. "It is possible," replies his Uncle with great calmness.

COMMENT: The Marquis Saint Evrémonde (for such is the family name that both he and his nephew share) is out of favor with the court and has been for some years through some happening of which we at this time have no inkling. But the mention of the *lettre de cachet,* which we have already heard of and which the Marquis would not hesitate to use to rid himself of his nephew if it lay in his power to do so, recalls to us the case of Dr. Manette. The mention of it here is not a coincidence, for it will be revealed that Dr. Manette's imprisonment and the Marquis' disfavor at court have much to do with one another.

It is true that such "instruments of correction" are not within his power, says the Marquis, but then the nobles have lost many privileges. Charles comments that the name Saint Evrémonde is probably the most detested name in France, but his uncle is not to be softened by such an approach. "Let us hope so," he says. "Detestation of the high is the involuntary homage of the low." Charles presses his point. "We have done wrong and are reaping the fruits of wrong. Even in my father's time we did a world of wrong, injuring every human creature who came between us and our pleasure, whatever it was." Charles is bound to a system that is frightful to him and, to execute his mother's dying wish, to redress the wrongs committed by his family, he seeks assistance and power, in vain. "Seeking them from me, my nephew, you will for ever seek them in vain, be assured," his uncle replies. "My friend, I will die perpetuating the system under which I have lived." There is no point in continuing the conversation. Charles renounces his property and France altogether and vows to start again in England under his new name, for England is his refuge. "They say," comments his uncle, "that it is the refuge of many. You know a compatriot who has found a refuge there? A doctor? With a daughter?" Charles answers yes and wishes to question his uncle further on this comment but the audience is at an end and his uncle bids his good night.

As the sun rises the next day people go about their tasks as they have done for ages. But the routine of the morning is disturbed by the ringing of the great bell at the chateau and the hurried figures everywhere. The mender of roads gathers with the populace at the fountain in the village to ponder these events, and we hear what has caused all this frenzy. For the Gorgon has cast her glance at the chateau once again during the night and one more stone face has been added there. It lay back on the pillow of the Marquis and through the heart of this stone figure a knife has been driven. Round its hilt is a piece of paper on which is scrawled, "Drive him fast to his tomb. This, from Jacques."

COMMENT: The Marquis shows during the conversation that he knows of Dr. Manette and Lucie, which confirms that connection with Dr. Manette's imprisonment that has already been suggested. Charles Darnay, who has come once again from England to plead with his uncle to help alleviate the sufferings of the peasantry, is rebuffed by the Marquis, for the Marquis is certain that his way of life will endure, and he feels no sympathy for the downtrodden masses. But in the space of a few hours the first crack appears in this monolithic caste, for the Marquis is slain in his bed and the note, signed "Jacques," clearly indicates that the perpetrator of this murder is a member of that militant group which will shortly plunge France into Revolution. And this death of a hated nobleman is but the first of many to come.

CHAPTER 10.   TWO PROMISES

It is a year after the death of the Marquis. Charles Darnay has established himself in England as a tutor of the French language and of French literature. With great perserverance and untiring industry he has prospered at this new employment. He spends part of his time at Cambridge University and the rest in London. His love for Lucie Manette has grown, a love which was born in that moment of danger at his trial. But he has never spoken a word of his love to anyone, including Lucie, until this day and, as he knows that Lucie is out walking with Miss Pross, he resolves to broach the subject to Dr. Manette and learn of his feelings on the subject. As he opens his heart to Dr. Manette, the doctor receives his words with obvious dread and what seems like actual pain. Darnay interprets this to mean that Dr. Manette fears a separation from Lucie if she should marry, but Charles assures him that he means to join this family and strengthen the bonds between Lucie and her father, not to tear them asunder. Dr. Manette believes him and promises that if Lucie ever reveals her love for Darnay to him that he would not stand in the way of their marriage. For, "if there were any apprehension, anything whatsoever, new or old, against the man she really loved — the direct responsibility thereof not lying on his head—they should all be obliterated for her sake." This heartfelt declaration is followed by silence, and fear and dread still haunt the doctor's expression.

Darnay then tells the doctor that he wishes to keep nothing back from him and desires to reveal his true name and the reasons for his being in England. "Stop!" The word explodes from Dr. Manette's lips and his hands rush to stop up his ears. "Tell me when I ask you, not now. If your suit should prosper, if Lucie should love you, you shall tell me on your marriage morning. Do you promise?" "Willingly." Darnay leaves before Lucie returns home. As she enters she hears a low hammering sound coming from her father's bedroom. Lucie goes to him and together they talk for a long time. She comes down from her bed later to look in upon his as he lies asleep. He sleeps heavily, and his shoemaking tools are all in their usual place.

COMMENT: The die is cast. Charles Darnay has revealed his love for Lucie to Dr. Manette, and the old feeling of fear and fore-

1) Dr. Not stop the marriage
2) On wedding day, Charles tell identity

boding has agitated the doctor as he hears the young man reveal his feelings. When Charles Darnay is about to disclose his history, the doctor stops him in dread of having his suspicions confirmed, for he suspects that this noble young man who loves his daughter is a member of that family whose name is most hated by him: Saint Evrémonde. But for his daughter's sake he summons up the courage to place her happiness before all other considerations, and if Charles and Lucie do love one another then they will be married with his blessing. But until that day should come he does not wish to have his suspicions confirmed. The turmoil in his mind causes him to return to his shoemaker's trade in the night and only Lucie's care and love eases him. Soon, that day *will* come and the awful truth will be revealed to Dr. Manette, and once again the cloud will descend upon him.

CHAPTER 11. A COMPANION PICTURE

Once again Stryver and Sydney Carton have spent the night working on legal briefs. Carton has been laboring every night for many nights in succession to clear up these papers for Stryver before the long vacation. At last they are finished and he pulls off the wet towel from his forehead and begins making another bowl of punch. Stryver then announces to Carton that he intends to marry. After much delaying, during which he criticizes Sydney for his anti-social manner and remarks that he, Stryver, is much more agreeable in a woman's society than Sydney, he announces the name of the lady whom he plans to honor with his proposal of marriage: Lucie Manette. The mention of the name has no outward effect on Sydney's composure except for the fact that he increases his consumption of punch. Stryver continues, praising his own virtues to his friend and making clear that he feels that all he has to do is announce his interest and Miss Manette will rush to wed him, for, after all, he says, "she will have in me a man already well off, and a rapidly rising man, and a man of some distinction: it is a piece of good fortune for her, but she is worthy of good fortune." After this recital of the advantages to be had in marrying him, Stryver falls to lecturing Carton again in a patronizing manner, which makes Stryver even more offensive than he has already been. "Marry. Provide somebody to take care of you. . . . Find out somebody and marry her. That's the kind of thing for *you*. Now think of it, Sydney." "I'll think of it," replies Sydney.

COMMENT: The pompous Mr. Stryver has decided that he will marry Lucie Manette. In his practical, logical mind he has considered the move and has decided that Lucie will be given the honor of being his wife, for after all, is he not a splendid catch for a woman? Sydney Carton manages to contain his true emotions on being informed of Stryver's intentions, for he probably knows that Stryver's chances with Lucie are as doomed to failure as his own would be, though for quite different reasons. So he holds his peace and waits for Stryver to be rudely awakened, as he will be by Mr. Lorry in the next chapter.

(Mr. Lorry)

CHAPTER 12.   THE FELLOW OF DELICACY

After some thought, Mr. Stryver decides to make Lucie's good fortune known to her before he leaves town for the long vacation. He has not a doubt as to the strength of his case—it is a plain case, and has not a weak spot in it. On his way to the Manette's lodgings to announce himself to Lucie, he passes Tellson's Bank and it enters his mind to divulge his intentions to Mr. Lorry who is, as he knows, a close friend of the Manettes. He enters the bank and greets Mr. Lorry in a booming voice which causes the clerks to look up with displeasure at him. Mr. Lorry, discreet as always, greets him quietly in his best business manner and inquires if there is anything he can do for Mr. Stryver. Nothing in a business way, replies Mr. Stryver, for he has come for a private visit and, so saying, he announces his plan to marry Lucie Manette. "Oh, dear me!" cries Mr. Lorry, rubbing his chin and looking dubious. "Oh dear me, Sir?" repeats Stryver. "Oh dear you, Sir? What may your meaning be, Mr. Lorry?" Mr. Lorry stammers for a bit and to Stryver's questions, "Am I not eligible?" "prosperous?" "advancing?" he assents readily. Well, then? Mr. Stryver is crestfallen and cannot understand Mr. Lorry's hesitation. The case is plain and Mr. Lorry, of all people, being a man of business, should see it. When Mr. Lorry suggests that Stryver is utterly beside himself, and Mr. Lorry becomes somewhat heated himself when the lawyer casts aspersions on Lucie. Finally, after much discussion, Mr. Lorry persuades Stryver to accept him as an emissary, to gauge the lay of the land, to sound out Lucie on the matter and thus avoid embarrassment to all concerned. Mr. Stryver then bursts out of Tellson's, and it finally dawns on him that there may be some reason for Mr. Lorry's moral certainty that Lucie would refuse him. He determines to take the offensive and put everyone else in the wrong. Accordingly, when Mr. Lorry stops by Mr. Stryver's chamber later in the evening to tell what he has found out, Mr. Stryver seems preoccupied as if he did not know why Mr. Lorry had come by, even though the meeting was prearranged. Finally, Mr. Lorry informs the lawyer that his suspicions were correct and that Mr. Stryver ought not press his suit any further. Mr. Stryver is very offhand about it, suggests that it was a momentary lapse that made him even consider proposing to Miss Manette, thanks Mr. Lorry for his good offices and rushes him out into the night before the gentleman from Tellson's knows what has happened.

COMMENT: Mr. Stryver, as a good lawyer should, manages to turn events that are going strongly against him to his own best use. He has accepted the fact of Lucie's rejection of his suit, although he still cannot understand the reason for her doing so, and he has made it seem as though everyone else was in the wrong in the whole affair. This suitor is now out of the way, and the stage is left clear for Charles Darnay.

(Carton)

CHAPTER 13. THE FELLOW OF NO DELICACY

Sydney Carton, like Charles Darnay, is a frequent visitor in the Manette household. But when there he is moody and morose and he very seldom pierces through the cloud that overshadows him. Still, the house and its occupants have a great attraction for him, and, often, in the dead of night he walks in the neighborhood of the Manette's.

On a pleasant day in August, Sydney Carton once again heads for the Manette house, but this time with an air of resolution. He finds Lucie at home alone at her work. She has never been quite at ease with him and the strange look about him on this occasion prompts her to ask him if he is well. He replies, "No. But the life I lead is not conducive to health. What is to be expected of, or by, such profligates." "Is it not a pity to live no better life?" Lucie asks. He agrees that it is a pity. "Then why not change it?" "It is too late for that. I shall never be better than I am. I shall sink lower, and be worse." Carton, in his despair, breaks down and weeps. Lucie is much distressed and he asks her forgiveness and begs her to hear him out. "I wish you to know," he continues, "that you have been the last dream of my soul. Since I knew you, I have been troubled by a remorse that I thought would never reproach me again. . . . I have had unformed ideas of striving afresh, beginning anew, shaking off sloth and sensuality, and fighting out the abandoned fight. A dream, all a dream, that ends in nothing, and leaves the sleeper where he lay down, but I wish you to know that you inspired it." "Will nothing of it remain? O Mr. Carton, think again! Try again!" "No. Miss Manette . . . I distress you; I draw fast to an end. Will you let me believe, when I recall this day, that the last confidence of my life was reposed in your pure and innocent breast, and that it lies there alone, and will be shared by no one?" "If that will be a consolation to you, yes," Lucie replies. "Thank you and God bless you." As he moves toward the door Sydney Carton promises that he will never return to this conversation again by so much as a passing word. "My last supplication of all, is this; and with it, I will relieve you of a visitor with whom I well know you have nothing in common . . . For you, and for any dear to you, I would do anything . . . I would embrace any sacrifice for you and for those dear to you ... Think now and then that there is a man who would give his life, to keep a life you love beside you," and with these words he leaves her.

> **COMMENT:** We see Sydney Carton here as a very different man from what we are used to seeing. His love for Lucie Manette, which he has carried in his breast since he first saw her at the trial, has lain hidden and only now does he reveal it to Lucie; not to ask for her hand but only to tell her that she has brightened his life and that if anyone could have rehabilitated him she could have. But he knows that to aspire to Lucie is hopeless, and he only asks that she think kindly of him and remember that he would do anything for her and for those she loves, even to laying down his life. Sydney Carton does not realize how prophetic he is being in this statement, for the opportunity for just such a demonstration of his devotion to Lucie will soon arise.

CHAPTER 14. THE HONEST TRADESMAN

It is Jerry Cruncher's habit, while waiting for an errand for Tellson's Bank, to sit with his son on a stool outside the bank and observe the comings and goings in Fleet Street, and occasionally to help an old lady across the street and receive a coin for his trouble. But there are precious few old ladies these days and few errands to run and, in general, his affairs are so unprosperous as to cause him to think that Mrs. Cruncher has been "flopping" again. As he sits there Jerry notices a noisy crowd approaching and he perceives that they are accompanying a funeral. As the crowd draws near, a hearse and a mourning coach, in which there sits a solitary mourner, can be seen and the crowd is shouting "Spies" and hissing and deriding the man riding in the coach. Funerals at all times hold an attraction for Jerry Cruncher and a funeral that attracts so much attention as this one does excites him greatly. After stopping several members of the crowd to inquire about this funeral, he learns that the deceased is Roger Cly, who was a spy for the Old Bailey. Jerry remembers that he saw the man before as a witness at Charles Darnay's trial. The crowd mobs the vehicles, forcing them to stop and they lay hands on the solitary mourner who just manages to get away after shedding his cloak and hat which the crowd tears to pieces with great enjoyment. Someone then suggests that the crowd accompany the coffin to the burial ground and, this suggestion being received with great joy, they all, with Jerry Cruncher among them, commandeer the coach and hearse and proceed to the burial ground where the coffin of Roger Cly is laid to rest, midst great rejoicing. Looking for new amusement, the mob breaks some windows and maltreats passerby until a rumor that the guards are coming causes them to disperse. Jerry Cruncher, having remained at the churchyard, remembers that Roger Cly was a young, well-made man, and he pays a call on his medical adviser — a distinguished surgeon — on his way back to Tellson's. When he arrives at the bank, young Jerry tells his father that there were no jobs in his absence and, as the bank closes, the two go home to tea.

At home Jerry Cruncher gives one more warning to his wife against her "flopping," and tells her that if his ventures go wrong tonight he will know that she has been praying against him and he will beat her for it just as if he'd seen her doing it. Young Jerry asks to go out with his father but is forbidden to do so. "I'm a going — as your mother knows — a fishing. That's where I'm going to. Going a fishing." "Your fishing rod gets rayther rusty; don't it, father?" "Never you mind," replies his father. During the remainder of the evening, Jerry keeps his wife in conversation through his constant grumbling, to prevent her from meditating any prayers to his disadvantage. Finally, young Jerry is put to bed and at about one o'clock in the morning the elder Jerry opens a locked cupboard and brings forth a sack, a crowbar, a rope and chain, and other fishing tackle of that nature, extinguishes the light, and goes out. Young Jerry, who has gone to bed fully clothed, follows his father out in order to study his father's mysterious honest calling. Following at some distance, young Jerry sees his parent meet two other men and follows them to a churchyard where the three scale the wall. Watching from outside the gate, young Jerry sees the three dig up a grave and, after much labor, succeed in raising a coffin to the surface. The sight is too much for him, and he runs all the way home and scrambles into bed. The next morning the elder Jerry Cruncher is in a foul mood and he starts the day by knocking his wife's head on the headboard of the bed. "You oppose yourself to the profit of the business and me and my partners suffer. You was to honour and obey; why the devil don't you?" There is not much food for breakfast and Jerry remains out of temper as he and his son set off to Tellson's bank. As they walk young Jerry asks "Father, what's a Resurrection-Man?" "He's a tradesman," replies his father. "His goods is a branch of scientific goods." "Person's bodies, ain't it, father? Oh, father, I should so like to be a Resurrection-Man when I'm quite growed up!" Jerry Cruncher's mood is soothed by his son's laudable intention, and he begins to think that his offspring may yet grow up to be a blessing to him and compensate him for his mother.

COMMENT: It is now revealed to us what Jerry's night occupation is. He and his associates dig up bodies from graveyards and sell them to medical men for scientific experimentation. But once again he has met with little success; for what reason we do not know. After all, we know that Roger Cly's body was buried, with

Jerry Cruncher in attendance, just this afternoon and we know that Cly was a perfect speciment for a surgeon's experimentation. But something *has* gone wrong with Jerry's "fishing," and Mrs. Cruncher has borne the blame for his lack of success. We are to learn more of this night's work later when Miss Pross' brother, Solomon, is confronted with Jerry's evidence concerning Roger Cly and is persuaded to help Sydney Carton in his plan to carry out the promise he made to Lucie Manette.

Casket was empty

CHAPTER 15.   KNITTING

The scene is once again Defarge's wine-shop in Paris. The drinking has begun early today as it has on the two previous days. But the wine does not lighten the spirit of the drinkers. Instead, it makes them gloomy and any fire that it instills in the breasts of the drinkers remains there and smolders. Indeed, there are many in the shop who cannot afford even a glass of wine, and these quench their thirst with talk as they glide from seat to seat at the tables in the shop. There is an air of preoccupation about the place, and games of cards and dominoes languish for want of interest by the players. Despite the unusual crowd of people in the wine-shop, the proprietor is not to be seen. However, nobody inquires after him, and no one is surprised to see only Madame Defarge in her seat at the counter, distributing the wine and taking in a few, small, battered coins.

At midday two men enter the shop, dusty and thirsty: one is the proprietor Defarge, the other is the mender of roads who saw the man hanging beneath the Marquis' carriage. No one speaks as they enter, though all eyes fasten on them. "Good-day, gentlemen!" says Monsieur Defarge. "It is bad weather, gentlemen." Every man looks at his neighbor and then casts down his eyes and sits silent. One man gets up and goes out. Defarge introduces the mender of roads, called "Jacques," to his wife and bids her to give him some wine. As Jacques drinks his wine and chews on a crust of dark bread that he has carried in his blouse, two more men get up and go out. When he has finished his repast, Defarge says to him "Come, then! You shall see the apartment that I told you you could occupy. It will suit you to a marvel." The two men leave the shop, enter a courtyard, and climb a steep staircase to a garret — the same garret where we have once before seen a whit-haired man making shoes, and as they reach the garret room there are the same three men who once observed the shoemaker at work. They are introduced by Defarge to the newcomer as Jacques One, Jacques Two and Jacques Three, Defarge himself being Jacques Four and the new arrival, the mender of roads, Jacques Five. Defarge tells Jacques Five to relate his story to the others. He begins by recounting the incident of the Marquis' coach and the man hanging beneath it. Then he picks up the thread of his narrative about a year later when he sees soldiers leading this same tall man to a prison near his village. The man has been sought all this time and finally has been captured. It is Gaspard, whose child was trampled beneath the hooves of the Marquis' horses and who has been arrested and charged with the murder of the Marquis. All the village dreams of the unhappy one high up in his prison cell, never to come out, except to die. The four men listen to the story with rapt attention and exchange dark glances with one another. Jacques Five continues his story: a rumor goes about the village that a petition has been presented to the king saying that Gaspard was maddened by the death of his child and that because of the petition his life will be spared. "Listen, then, Jacques," interrupts Jacques One. "Know that a petition *was* presented to the King and Queen. It is Defarge whom you see here, who, at the hazard of his life, darted out before the horses, with the petition in his hand." The story continues: Many rumors go about the village concerning the fate of the prisoner, some saying that he will be freed, some that he will be horribly tortured before being executed. At last, one Sunday night when all the village is asleep, soldiers and workmen come down from the prison and the workmen dig and hammer while the soldiers laugh and sing, and when the sun rises in the morning, there, by the fountain, poisoning the water, is a gallows forty feet high. All work stops and all the people assemble there. At midday, to the roll of drums, soldiers march out of the prison leading the prisoner and he is hanged on the gallows and left there for all the villagers to see and take a lesson from. As he finishes his story Jacques Five is asked to wait outside while the others deliberate. "How say you, Jacques?" Number One asks of Defarge. "To be registered as doomed to destruction," replies Defarge. "The chateau and all the race." "Magnificent," croaks Jacques Three who chews his fingers, trying to satisfy a craving that is for neither food nor drink.

COMMENT: The name of Saint Evrémonde and all members of the family are doomed to destruction and their names are to be inscribed in the register — the register kept by Madame Defarge as she knits. In each stitch she has noted down the name and crimes of those who are to be exterminated when the Revolution has come. The list is already long and Madame is kept busy constantly adding new names to it. With the addition of the House of Saint Evrémonde to her register, Charles Darnay's life becomes forfeit if he should ever set foot in France again. And the relentless workings of fate will see to it that he does return to his native land and set in motion the terrible sequel to this rash act which will involve all those we have already met in the course of the story, excepting Mr. Stryver.

Defarge announces to his fellow conspirators that he will take Jacques Five, the mender of roads, to see the King and Queen at Versailles on Sunday. "What?" exclaims the hungry man, Jacques Three, staring. "Is it a good sign, that he wishes to see Royalty and Nobility?" "Jacques," replies Defarge, "judiciously show a cat milk, if you wish her to thirst for it. Judiciously show a dog his natural prey, if you wish him to bring it down one day." With this the meeting comes to an end.

When Sunday comes, the Defarges and the mender of roads make their trip to Versailles in a public conveyance. All the way there, Madame Defarge knits, and in answer to a fellow passenger's question as to what she is knitting, her reply is "shrouds." The arrival of the King and Queen and the court throws the mender of roads into raptures and he yells himself hoarse cheering the Royal House. Later, he regrets his lapse, but Defarge is pleased. "You are the fellow we want. You make these fools believe that it will last forever. Then, they are the more insolent, and it is the nearer ended." Madame Defarge questions the mender of roads. If he were shown a great heap of dolls and a flock of birds and were set upon them to strip them for his own advantage, he would set upon the richest and gayest dolls and the birds with the finest feathers, would he not? "It is true, Madame." "You have seen both dolls and birds today," says Madame Defarge. "Now go home!"

> **COMMENT:**   The slaying of the Marquis by Gaspard has led to his capture and execution. The body is left hanging in public to serve as a lesson, but instead it will serve as a reminder of oppression and misery. In the cravings of Jacques Three we see the blood-lust which is soon to transform the entire populace. In a short while even the mender of roads who has cheered the Royal family will fear and rend and despoil the enemies of the people, intoxicated by the smell of blood.

CHAPTER 16.   STILL KNITTING

The Defarges return home to Saint Antoine while the mender of roads goes on his way. They stop at the guard station where Monsieur Defarge alights and chats with the soldiers and the police there, one of whom he knows quite well. As the Defarges proceed on their way, Madame asks her husband what news has been gathered from his friend. The news is that a new spy has been commissioned for the Saint Antoine quarter. He is English and his name is John Barsad. Madame Defarge makes a mental note of his name and his description, and promises to add him to her register in the morning.

testified against Darnay

COMMENT: John Barsad, who testified at Charles Darnay's trial in London, is now in Paris, still a spy but with a new allegiance: the French Government. His presence in France will shortly be explained more fully, and we shall soon learn more of his history and of his true identity.

Madame Defarge arranges the accounts in the wine-shop before they retire and she notices a look of fatigue in her husband's face. "I am a little tired," Defarge admits. "You are faint of heart tonight, my dear," Madame Defarge comments. "Well then, it is a long time." "It is a long time," repeats his wife, "and when is it not a long time? Vengeance and retribution require a long time; it is the rule. I tell thee that although it is a long time on the road, it is on the road and coming. I tell thee it never retreats, and never stops. When the time comes, let loose a tiger and a devil; but wait for the time with the tiger and the devil chained — not shown — yet always ready."

Next day Madame Defarge is at her usual place in the wine-shop, knitting, when a stranger enters. Madame fastens a rose on her hair, and as she does so, the customers that are there drift out one by one, so casually that an observer would not notice that a signal had caused their departure. The newcomer is John Barsad and he and Madame Defarge exchange a few pleasantries as he sips his cognac. As they chat, customers who enter the shop see the rose in Madame Defarge's hair and leave immediately. While she talks with Barsad, Madame is knitting his name into her register. Barsad tries to trap her into admitting some discontent with the present order, but she neatly avoids the pitfalls that he lays for her. Barsad brings up Gaspard's execution and mentions that he believes that there is much compassion and anger in the district because of it. Madame states that she is unaware of such feelings. At this point, Defarge enters and Barsad greets him with "Good day, Jacques." Defarge corrects him: his name is Ernest, not Jacques. Barsad takes another tack. He mentions that he is acquainted with the Manettes in England and knows the part that Defarge has played in helping them out of France. Defarge does not deny it, but Madame informs the spy that since their safe arrival in England there has been little word of them. The spy continues along this line. He tells them that Miss Manette is to be married to the nephew of the late Marquis, a Mr. Charles Darnay as he is known in England. Madame Defarge knits steadily but this information has a palpable effect on Monsieur Defarge and his hand is unsteady as he lights his pipe. The spy notes this and records it in his mind. Having scored this one hit, Barsad pays for his cognac and leaves. Defarge is shaken by this new development. "Is is not very strange that, after all our sympathy for Monsieur her father and herself, her husband's name should be proscribed under your hand at this moment, by the side of that infernal dog's who has just left us?" "Her husband's destiny will take him where he is to go, and will lead him to the end that is to end him. That is all I know," Madame Defarge says with her usual composure. She rolls up her knitting and removes the rose from her hair, and the wine-shop gradually fills again.

In the evening the women of the district are all to be seen sitting on doorsteps and window-ledges. They are knitting, knitting to keep their hands busy — the mechanical work serves as a substitute for eating and drinking, it eases the hunger pangs. Madame Defarge goes from group to group while her husband watches her admiringly: "A great woman, a strong woman, a frightfully grand woman!" The fingers, the eyes and the thoughts of the women go quicker and fiercer as Madame Defarge passes. It will not be long before they will be seated around a new instrument called La Guillotine and will knit as they count the dropping heads.

> **COMMENT:** Ernest Defarge, as strong as he is in his determination for revenge and retribution, pales when seen beside his wife. Madame Defarge has an all-consuming hatred of the nobility, a hatred which stems from the very same incident which led to Dr. Manette's imprisonment. The news of Lucie Manette's impending marriage to Charles Darnay softens Defarge slightly because of his old relationship with Dr. Manette, but Madame Defarge is implacable: if the nephew of the hated Marquis comes to France, his head will roll just like the rest of them. There is something menacing about her, for she will not rest until her thirst for vengeance is slaked and her very presence among the women quickens their mood and sharpens their determination. Madame Defarge will not be stopped until she comes face to face with an Englishwoman whose determination and strength are as great as her own, but whose heart is strengthened by love, an emotion which it is difficult to believe exists in the heart of Madame Defarge.

CHAPTER 17. ONE NIGHT

It is the eve of Lucie Manette's wedding day. Lucie has reserved this last evening for her father and they are sitting under the plane-tree in the garden. Lucie is radiantly happy, but she is a little uneasy about her father's reactions to the marriage. He reassures her that her marriage will not injure their relationship. "My future is far brighter, Lucie, seen through your marriage, than it could have been without it." For the first time he speaks of his time of imprisonment and recalls that he often thought about his daughter and imagined her married and her home full of remembrances of her dear father. This thought comforted him in his long trial. Lucie is warmed by his sincere love for her and they embrace and go into the house.

The marriage is to take place in the morning; only Miss Pross and Mr. Lorry are to be there. Some rooms on an upper floor have been rented so that Charles and Lucie and Dr. Manette can live together. Dr. Manette is cheerful during supper and drinks to the absent Charles. Late at night, Lucie comes to her father's room, an unknown fear making her restless. But Dr. Manette is sleeping peacefully. Lucie kisses him and goes out.

> COMMENT: Dr. Manette has resolved his doubts to a great degree and he wishes only for Lucie's happiness. Still, there is some fear lurking in him and Lucie is aware of it, despite his outward composure. Tomorrow, on her wedding day, Lucie's husband-to-be is to come to Dr. Manette and reveal his name and history; and the fear that has brought Lucie down tonight to look in on her father is to be made manifest and the cloud is to descend over Dr. Manette's face once more.

CHAPTER 18.   NINE DAYS

The wedding day has dawned bright and clear. All is in readiness, and Lucie, Mr. Lorry, and Miss Pross are waiting to go to the church; there to wait for Charles Darnay and Mr. Manette who are closeted in the doctor's room. Mr. Lorry remarks on Lucie's beauty and he and Miss Pross both shed a tear of happiness over the coming nuptials. The door of the doctor's room opens and Dr. Manette comes out with Charles Darnay. Manette's face is deadly pale but he remains outwardly composed. They all proceed to the church in two carriages, and soon Charles Darnay and Lucie Manette are married. Everyone returns home for breakfast and then Lucie and Dr. Manette embrace and Charles and Lucie depart. Mr. Lorry notices that a great change has come over the doctor. The old scared lost look is on his face and he absently clasps his head and wanders into his own room. Mr. Lorry suggests to Miss Pross that they not disturb him. He, Mr. Lorry, must look in at Tellson's, but he will be back shortly, and then he and Miss Pross will take the doctor for a ride in the country.

Mr. Lorry's business at Tellson's Bank takes him longer than he'd planned, and when he returns two hours later, he hears a low sound of knocking coming from the doctor's room. "Good God, what is that." Miss Pross is suddenly at hand. a terrified look on her face. "O me, O me! All is lost! What is to be told to Ladybird? He doesn't know me, and is making shoes!" Mr. Lorry hurries into the Doctor's room. "Doctor Manette. My dear friend, Doctor Manette!" But the mist is over the Doctor's eyes once again and there is no recognition there. He continues making shoes, and nothing that Mr. Lorry says can recall him to his normal state. The only hope Mr. Lorry can see is a look of perplexity in the doctor's eyes, as if he were trying to resolve something in his mind. A course of action is decided upon: it is essential that news of Dr. Manette's relapse be kept from Lucie and from all who know him. To this end word is to be given out that the doctor is unwell and requires a few days of complete rest. Meanwhile, Miss Pross is to write to Lucie and inform her that her father has been called away professionally, to explain why she won't receive any communications from him. Mr. Lorry makes arrangements to absent himself from Tellson's in order that he may remain near the doctor and watch for any change in his condition. He and Miss Pross divide the night into two watches and observe him from an adjoining room.

And so the days pass and Mr. Lorry begins to lose hope of his old friend's recovery. At dusk on the ninth evening, the shoemaker's hand has never seemed more nimble and expert.

> **COMMENT:** The revelations of Charles Darnay have brought back all the old terrors and fears of his days of imprisonment to Dr. Manette. His mind, torn between his desire for his daughter's happiness and the fear and hatred he feels toward his old enemies, has been cast into the blackness from which it seems he will never recover. But such is the power of the human psyche that even this great shock will fade and Dr. Manette will be restored to his faculties and will live to see this newly-married couple torn apart and his daughter's new-found happiness threatened by an old document of his, written when he was "One Hundred and Five, North Tower."

CHAPTER 19.   AN OPINION

On the tenth morning after Dr. Manette's relapse, Mr. Lorry is awakened by the sunlight shining into the room where he has fallen asleep during his nightly vigil. Going to the doctor's room, he sees that the shoemaker's bench and tools are put aside again and Dr. Manette sits reading at the window. At breakfast all is as it was before Lucie's wedding and there appears to be no remebrance on the part of Dr. Manette of his nine days of oblivion. Mr. Lorry resolves to discuss the case with Dr. Manette after breakfast. He presents the problem to the doctor as if the person under discussion were some other friend. Doctor Manette understands what has happened and asks Mr. Lorry to spare no details in recounting the circumstances of his relapse. When Mr. Lorry has done so, Dr. Manette is thoughtful for a while and then he offers his opinion on the case: the relapse was caused by a revival of the train of thought and remembrance that was the first cause of the malady. An intense association of a distressing nature was recalled, and though he dreaded such a reawakening, his efforts to prepare himself for it had been in vain. But the worst is over, Dr. Manette believes, and only an extraordinary jarring of that familiar chord could renew the disorder. Mr. Lorry is somewhat relieved, but not altogether. However, Dr. Manette's confident belief gives Mr. Lorry the courage to broach another question: Would it not be best to remove the shoemaker's equipment? Is it not a concession to the misgiving to keep the bench and tools? A great struggle is seen taking place in the doctor's mind, but in the end he gives his permission. When Dr. Manette shortly departs to join Lucie and Charles, as has been previously arranged, Mr. Lorry, in the night, hacks the shoemaker's bench to pieces and burns the fragment in the kitchen fire and the tools and leather are buried in the garden. Miss Pross and Mr. Lorry look, and feel, like accomplices in a horrible crime as they go about this deed.

COMMENT: Dr. Manette has been restored to himself, and in his own mind there is very little chance that such a relapse will take place again. His newly-gained assurance is weakened momentarily when Mr. Lorry asks his permission to destroy the shoemaker's equipment, but finally he sanctions it. And there *is* a new strength in him, a strength which will grow and which will be put to use in the defense of his son-in-law before the tribunal of the Jacquerie in Paris.

CHAPTER 20. A PLEA

Lucie and Charles Darnay have not been home for more than a few hours when Sydney Carton appears at their house to offer his congratulations. Carton takes Darnay to one side and in an earnest manner, unusual in him, asks Darnay if they might be friends. He recalls the evening after the trial. "On the drunken occasion in question, I was insufferable about liking you, and not liking you, I wish you would forget it." Darnay replies, "I declare to you on the faith of a gentleman, that I have long dismissed it from my mind. Have I had nothing more important to remember in the great service you rendered me that day?" "As to the great service," says Carton, "I am bound to avow to you, when you speak of it in that way, that it was mere professional claptrap.

I don't know that I cared what became of you, when I rendered it. — Mind! I say when I rendered it; I am speaking of the past."

> **COMMENT:** He is speaking of the past, before his conversation with Lucie. Now that Charles is loved by Lucie, Carton cares very much what happens to Darnay and will prove that he cares in the shadow of the guillotine.

Carton also asks if he might have the privilege of coming and going at odd times in the Darnay household — it is doubtful that he would take advantage of it more than four times a year. Darnay readily agrees and they shake hands and Carton leaves.

Charles Darnay touches upon this conversation during the evening and speaks of Carton as a problem of carelessness and recklessness and later, as he and Lucie prepare to retire, Lucie gently asks her husband not to be so hard on Sydney Carton. "I would ask you to believe that he has a heart he very, very seldom reveals, and that there are deep wounds in it. My dear, I have seen it bleeding." Her husband is quite astounded at this and regrets that he has been inconsiderate in speaking of Carton. Lucie continues, "I fear he is not to be reclaimed; there is scarcely a hope that anything in his character or fortunes is reparable now. But, I am sure that he is capable of good things, gentle things, even magnanimous things." And Charles Darnay kisses away the tears of pity that fall from her soft blue eyes.

> **COMMENT:** As he revealed himself in a new light to Lucie, Carton now speaks with her husband in a manner quite unusual with him. The enmity which Carton once felt towards Darnay is now gone and they are now bound in friendship, though Carton will seldom visit the Darnay home. Lucie is once again prophetic when she speaks of Carton's being capable of magnanimous things.

CHAPTER 21.   ECHOING FOOTSTEPS

The years pass for Lucie, and there is happiness and sorrow in equal measure. Lucie gives birth to a daughter, also called Lucie, and the tread of her tiny feet and the sound of her prattling words fill the house with sunshine. A little boy is then born to her but he dies young and the rustling of an Angel's wings are blended with the other echoes in the house. And life goes on.

Sydney Carton, true to his word, seldom comes to visit. Six times a year at most he comes uninvited and sits with the family through the evening. On these occasions he is always sober. Carton is the first stranger to whom little Lucie holds out her chubby arms and he remains close to her as she grows up. Stryver meanwhile shoulders his way through the law, dragging his useful friend, Carton, in his wake. Stryver has married a rich widow with three sons, and is fond of telling Mrs. Stryver, over his glass of wine, of the wiles Mrs. Darnay once used to catch him, but he was not to be caught.

The echoes from France are beginning to rumble ominously, and one night in mid-July, 1789, Mr. Lorry arrives late at the Darnay household. He has had a hectic day at Tellson's. The storm brewing in France has caused a run upon Tellson's, for the French customers of the bank are eager to entrust their property to the firm's safekeeping. "That has a bad look," says Charles Darnay who saw this storm coming long ago.

The scene then shifts to France and the Saint Antoine quarter of Paris. The time has come and the multitudes of scarecrows in the streets clutch for weapons which are handed out to them — blades, bayonets, muskets, powder and ball, axes, pikes — weapons of every description. Every pulse and heart in Saint Antoine is at high-fever beat. It is July 14th, a day which is to go down in history as Bastille Day, and the mob, centered around the wine-shop, with Monsieur and Madame Defarge at its head, pushes on to that fortress. The sea rises and with an unearthly roar the battle is joined. Smoke and fire are everywhere and in the forefront are Defarge, working as a cannoneer, and Madame Defarge, rallying the women, and carrying an axe with a pistol and knife at her waist. The women are variously armed but all armed alike in hunger and revenge. Gradually the furious living sea wears down the defenders of the Bastille and the fortress is taken! Defarge collars an old prison officer and commands him to lead him to One Hundred and Five, North Tower, the cell where Dr. Manette was imprisoned. The turnkey, Defarge, and Jacques Three hurry through the prison, fighting their way through the throngs. Defarge and Jacques Three ransack the cell where they can see, scratched on the wall, "A.M., a poor physician." They then retrace their steps and soon are swallowed up by the crowds. The governor of the Bastille has been taken, the man who symbolizes oppression to the thousands gathered there. The governor is borne along through the streets. As the crowd reaches its destination, he is attacked with a rain of stabs and blows, and as he falls dead, Madame Defarge places her foot on his neck and hews off his head. The crowd surges on, among the people seven prisoners of the Bastille newly releaesed and seven newly lopped-off heads mounted on pikes. There is no stopping them now. They are headlong, mad, and dangerous, and they are not easily pacified when once stained red.

COMMENT: The smoldering ashes have finally burst into flame and the flame engulfs everything in sight. The thirst for revenge has been too long suppressed and this thirst is being slaked with wholesale slaughter. The sight of a corpse swinging from a post or a head on a pike is a common one, and no one glories in the slaughter more than Madame Defarge. And this is only the beginning. The sea is still rising, and before long, there will be no one who is not swallowed up in it, either as a participant or a victim. The force of this sea will shortly draw Charles Darnay, and later his family, to Paris for the final act in this surging, bloody drama.

CHAPTER 22. THE SEA STILL RISES

It is a week after the Bastille has fallen. The scene is Defarge's wine-shop where once again Madame Defarge presides. There is no rose in her hair, for with the events of the past week no spy dares set foot in the neighborhood. There are too many street lamps nearby that might be used as gallows. Nearby is sitting one of Madame Defarge's sister-hood who, through her bloody participation in the week's events, has earned the nickname "The Vengeance." Suddenly Defarge himself rushes in, breathless: He has news. Foulon, an old aristocrat who was believed dead is discovered to be alive. He so feared for his life that he had staged a mock funeral, but the ruse has been discovered and the entire assembly shouts for his blood. His crime: he told the starving people that they might eat grass. The blood of the citizens begins to boil once again and The Vengeance runs from house to house arousing the women. The men grab their weapons and the throng, with the Defarges, The Vengeance, and Jacques Three in front, rushes to the Hotel de Ville where Foulon is being held captive. The crowd is in a frenzy now and Foulon is led from the building, torn, bruised and bleeding, begging for mercy. A noose is thrown over a lamppost and Foulon is hoisted up. The rope breaks. He is raised again, shrieking, and the rope breaks again. Finally, the third time the rope holds and shortly thereafter Foulon's head is upon a pike. Then the news reaches the crowd that Foulon's nephew, another enemy of the people, is coming into Paris under a guard five hundred strong. He is seized, despite his protection, and in a trice his head and heart are mounted on pikes and the three grisly objects are carried through the streets in a procession. Gradually, calm returns to the streets and the citizens return to their ragged children. Night falls over Saint Antoine. Defarge, as he closes up his shop, speaks to his wife: "At last it is come, my dear!" "Eh well!" answers Madame. "Almost."

COMMENT: A brief episode of calm after the fall of the Bastille and then the crowd is lusting after blood again. With each taste of blood, the intervals will become briefer until murder and pillage engulf France each hour, unceasingly. The revolution is only just getting under way. Madame Defarge's word "almost" indicates that the terror has not reached a peak high enough to please her. Much more will happen and many more lives will be drawn into the whirlpool of terror before her thirst can be slaked.

CHAPTER 23.   FIRE RISES

There is a change come over the village where Gaspard has been hanged. The prison overlooking the town does not seem as dominant as it once did — there are fewer soldiers stationed there and their commanding officers are not certain that the soldiers will obey any orders that they might give. And there are new faces to be seen, rough faces that speak strange dialects. These are members of the Jacquerie spreading to the four corners of France fomenting violence and sudden death wherever they go. One such meets the mender of roads as he works on the highway. They greet each other with the name "Jacques" and sit down to talk. The mender of roads gives some directions to the stranger who then lies down to take a nap. He has obviously traveled far, for his ankles are chafed and bleeding. The red cap he wears identifies him as a member of the Jacquerie. At sundown the mender of roads awakens him and the two men part.

When the village has taken its poor supper, the inhabitants do not retire as usual. A curious whispering has run through the town and all the people turn out of doors and assemble at the fountain. An air of expectancy hangs over them. Monsieur Gabelle, the village functionary, grows uneasy and sends word to the sacristan at the church that it may be necessary to ring the alarm bells by and by. At the chateau, four dark figures may be seen assembling in the courtyard. Suddenly, a light is seen in the chateau, and another, and another. Then flames burst forth from the windows. A servant dashes from the chateau and gallops down the hill to the village. "Help, Gabelle! Help everyone!" The alarm bell sounds but no help comes. The villagers stand about with folded arms, looking at the pillar of flame in the sky. "It must be forty feet high," they say (as high as Gaspard's gallows), and no one moves. The solitary rider gallops up to the prison and asks the officers to help. The officers look at the soldiers who look at the fire and give no orders. "It must burn," they answer.

The villagers, light-headed with the fire and this evidence of their new strength, recall that Monsieur Gabelle has to do with the collection of taxes and, surrounding his house, they order him to come out. Gabelle heavily bars his door and retires to his house-top behind his stack of chimneys, resolved if they come for him, to throw himself from the parapet. But the dawn finally comes and the people retire to their homes.

Similar events take place in other villages, on this night and on others, and everywhere the members of the Jacquerie are to be found fomenting unrest, setting fires, and awaking the populace to their new-found power and strength.

> **COMMENT:** The chateau, the symbol of oppression, is burned down and no one lifts a finger to save it. To such a low has the power of the nobility sunk. Although in individual villages the functionaries and soldiers are successful in bringing the villageres to heel, the trend is to local uprisings which the authorities are powerless to put down. And Monsieur Gabelle has been spared on this night so that he may act a role in the coming drama in being the magnet that draws Charles Darnay to France and into the hands of the Jacquerie.

CHAPTER 24.   DRAWN TO THE LOADSTONE ROCK

It is three years since the day of July 14th when the Bastille fell. In the intervening time the French nobility, those who were able to, have left their native land and scattered far and wide, many to England, with whatever possessions they were able to bring. In London, Tellson's Bank is a great gathering-place for the nobles. There they can pick up scraps of information that can be relied upon, and news of their fellows is exchanged there. Thus, Tellson's serves as a kind of High Exchange, and all inquiries concerning members of the French nobility or events in France are made there.

On a misty afternoon Mr. Lorry sits at his desk at Tellson's and Charles Darnay stands talking with him in a low voice. It develops that Mr. Lorry is planning a trip to Paris and Charles Darnay is attempting to dissuade him. Darnay, somewhat restless, remarks that he wishes he were going, thinking that somehow he might be listened to, and might have the power to persuade some restraint. Mr. Lorry must go to France to straighten out the affairs of Tellson's and to save what records and documents he can. All around the two men as the talk are nobles swarming about, boasting how they will avenge themselves on the people before long. This empty and absurd buzzing angers Darnay, particularly the buzzing of Mr. Stryver who is in the crowd expounding to the nobles his devices for exterminating the French people from the face of the earth.

At this point Mr. Lorry's superior brings a letter to his desk addressed to the Marquis Saint Evrémonde, entrusted to the care of Tellson's. Mr. Lorry replies that he has asked everyone there but no one knows of his whereabouts. Charles Darnay has noticed the name on the envelope. The reason of Mr. Lorry's ignorance of the presence of the Marquis Saint Evrémonde before him is the result of a pledge given to Dr. Manette on the day of Lucie's wedding that no one is to know of Charles' true identity until Dr. Manette himself dissolves the obligation. Not even Lucie knows of it. Darnay tells Mr. Lorry that he knows the Marquis and will deliver the letter.

Darnay withdraws to read it. It is from Gabelle. He has been imprisoned by the revolution and is soon to be brought before the tribunal, and will certainly lose his life unless the Marquis comes to help him. Charles Darnay reflects that despite his good intentions, he has not done all he might have for the suffering peasants on his estate. True, he had relinquished the rent and taxes that they had formerly paid to the chateau. But he should have systematically worked things out. And now, because he hadn't, the life of Gabelle will be forfeit, his only crime being that he served the interests of an emigrant nobleman. Darnay makes his decision: he must go to Paris to save Gabelle and to perhaps have some influence for good on the Revolution itself, because he had forfeited his estates and title willingly and had since earned his daily bread through the sweat of his brow.

The decision made, Darnay sets about to implement it. He returns to Tellson's to take leave of Mr. Lorry and he gives him a message to take to Gabelle. The message: "He has received the letter, and will come." He sees Mr. Lorry off, and that night sits up late writing two letters, one to Lucie, and one to Dr. Manette. In them he explains his reasons for going and tries to calm any fears they might have by saying that he is in no danger. He confides Lucie and his little daughter to Dr. Manette's care and promises to write when he has arrived in Paris. The next evening he bids Lucie goodbye, pretending that he is going out for but a moment, leaves his two letters with a porter for later delivery, and sets out on horseback for Dover and the boat to Paris.

COMMENT: The loadstone rock has exerted its force, and Charles Darnay is on his way to Paris. In the words of Madame Defarge, "Her husband's destiny will take him where he is to go, and will lead him to the end that is to end him." Fate has seen to it that he would see the letter addressed to him and fate has seen to it that he would not see any danger in his going to Paris. He will learn of his mistake very shortly when he is locked in the fortress of L'Abbaye to await trial before the tribunal as the Marquis St. Evrémonde, aristocrat and enemy of the people.

BOOK THE THIRD — THE TRACK OF A STORM

CHAPTER 1. IN SECRET

Traveling is difficult in France in 1792. In addition to the normal difficulties of bad roads and bad horses, the traveler must now contend with bands of citizen patriots who stop all travelers, question them, examine their papers, and either turn them back, send them on, or imprison them on the spot as suits their mood.

It becomes clear to Charles Darnay as he proceeds to Paris that there is no turning back until he is cleared as a good citizen in Paris. As the barriers drop behind him on the road the feeling that his freedom is completely gone strikes him. Until now, the showing of Gabelle's letter has gotten him through his obstacles but in a little town, still a long way from Paris, he is stopped again and the difficulties he encounters there convinces him that he has reached a crisis in his journey. As he lies asleep in a small inn to which he has been taken, he is awakened by a local functionary and three armed patriots who wear the familiar red caps on their heads. Darnay is informed by the functionary that he is to be sent to Paris under an escort and must pay for the escort himself. When Darnay protests, the answer is "Silence! Peace, aristocrat!" which is uttered by one of the patriots. "It is as the good patriot says," observes the functionary, timidly. "You are an aristocrat, and must have an escort."

Darnay sets out at three A.M., having paid a heavy price for his escort: two armed guards who ride on either side of him. Even as he rides with his escort, Darnay does not feel any fear as to the outcome of his journey. He is confident that when his testimony, and the testimony of Gabelle, is heard that he and his representative will both be freed.

> **COMMENT:** Even now, having taken into custody, Charles Darnay does not recognize his predicament. His basic goodness and the fact that he, too, objected to the excesses of the old regime he thinks will protect him from harm. But he depends too much on the value of calm and reason in a land where calm and reason have fled. And he has not reckoned with the venom of the Defarges.

As the three riders reach Beauvais, the streets are filled with people. The mood of the crowd is ominous and many voices call out, "Down with the emigrant." He begs them to hear him. "Emigrant, my friends! Do you not see me here, in France, of my own will?" "You are a cursed emigrant," answers a furious citizen, and you are a cursed aristocrat!" A decree is mentioned which makes Darnay's life forfeit to the people. When he inquires about this decree, he is told that there exists a decree for selling the property of emigrants; it was passed by the revolutionary tribunal on the day that Darnay left England. There arc other decrees planned — banishing all emigrants and condemning to death all who return.

Daylight finds Darnay and his two guards before the wall of Paris. A man in authority comes out and asks for Darnay's papers. As he looks at them he shows some surprise and stares at Darnay with close attention. He withdraws into the guard-house. While he is gone, Darnay observes that the gate is kept by a mixed guard of soldiers and patriots, the latter being more numerous. While they are free about letting people enter the gate, those wishing to leave are very carefully checked and those waiting in line to be passed often lay down on the ground to sleep or smoke until their turn comes. The man returns and requests Darnay to dismount and he gives to the guards a receipt. The two guards, leading Darnay's horse, turn back from the gate while Darnay is taken to the guard-house.

> **COMMENT:** Darnay's new escort is none other than Defarge himself. At last the Marquis Saint Evrémonde is delivered into the hands of the Revolution! But Defarge has some misgivings. After all, is not Darnay the husband of Lucie Manette, the child of Defarge's old master? But despite a momentary uncertainty, Defarge, through his own determination and the urgings of his wife, decides to exterminate this last member of an accursed line.

An officer receives Darnay and Defarge and questions the prisoner. After learning his identity, the officer announces, "You are consigned, Evrémonde, to the prison of La Force." To Darnay's expressions of protest the only reply is, "We have new laws, Evrémonde, and new offenses since you were here. Emigrants have no rights, Evrémonde." And on a paper that he hands to Defarge are written the words, "In Secret." As Defarge, Darnay, and the guards go out, Defarge asks Charles if he is truly the man who wed Lucie Manette. Darnay answers yes, and as Defarge seems to be concerned about his situation Darnay asks his help. Defarge utterly rejects the possibility for, after all, as Defarge says, "Other people have been similarly buried in worse prisons before now." "But never by me, Citizen Defarge." This answer causes Defarge to glare darkly at Darnay and after a moment he speaks again. "I will do nothing for you. My duty is to my country and the people. I am the sworn servant of both, against you. I will do nothing for you."

> **COMMENT:** Unwittingly, Charles Darnay has reminded Defarge even more strongly of his crime, or, more exactly, of the crimes of his family. This reminder solidifies Defarge's antagonism and seals Darnay's fate.

They walk through the streets and Darnay is struck by the fact that the sight of a nobleman being led to prison does not affect the townspeople at all. He hears an orator speaking to a crowd and learns that the King is in prison, and for the first time he realizes the danger to which he has voluntarily exposed himself. But even now he does not see his position as hopeless, for the mass executions by the guillotine have not yet begun and the frightful deeds which are to take place have not even formed in the minds of those who are to commit them.

Darnay and Defarge arrive at the gate of the prison of La Force. The gaoler (English spelling of jailer) grumbles about having to accommodate another prisoner. "In secret, too," he mutters as he looks at the paper Defarge has given him. Defarge departs and Darnay and the gaoler proceed through the prison, many doors locking behind him. The prison is gloomy, dark, and filthy, and the stench is almost overpowering. Finally, they come to a large, low chamber crowded with men and women. They seem like ghosts as they rise to greet the newcomer. Their manners are refined and elegant, and the ghosts of wit, pride, and frivolity hang over these prisoners as they welcome Darnay to this society of La Force prison. The gaolers in the chamber seem extraordinarily coarse by comparison with those they guard. A gentleman of courtly appearance asks Darnay if he is "in secret." "I do not understand the meaning of the term, but I have heard them say so." "Ah, what a pity! We so much regret it! I grieve to inform the society — in secret." A murmur of commiseration is heard as the gaoler leads Darnay to another door and the faces vanish behind him.

The door opens on a stone staircase, leading upward. When they climb forty steps (Darnay has counted them), they arrive at a low, black door behind which is a solitary cell. It is cold and damp, but not dark. In the cell are a chair, a table, and a straw mattress. After inspecting these objects, the gaoler leaves, telling Darnay that he will be visited and may buy his food, but nothing more. Charles Darnay begins pacing about the cell. "Five paces by four and a half, five paces by four and a half," he repeats over and over again and the words come to his mind — "He made shoes, he made shoes." As he paces faster the roar of the city outside the walls is intermingled with the wail of voices that he knows, rising above the roar.

COMMENT: Charles Darnay's destiny has brought him to Paris and to imprisonment at La Force. His hope that he might have some calming effect on the citizens of Paris have been dashed and he has been escorted to prison by the husband of Madame Defarge, his most implacable enemy who will stop at nothing to avenge herself on him. Darnay has now learned what the ominous words "in secret" mean: solitary confinement. And the irony lies in the fact that he is reliving the experience of Doctor Manette who was also consigned to prison "in secret" and by the hand of another Marquis Saint Evrémonde. Although he does not know the details of Doctor Manette's imprisonment, this irony is not lost on Charles Darnay, and the words, "he made shoes" remind him of it and of the method that Doctor Manette used to keep himself from losing his mind.

CHAPTER 2.   THE GRINDSTONE

The French branch of Tellson's is located in the Saint Germain quarter of Paris, in a house once occupied by the Monseigneur for whom four men prepared chocolate, the gentleman we met in an earlier chapter. Mr. Jarvis Lorry has occupied himself since his arrival in Paris in trying to preserve Tellson's records and to straighten out the tangled affairs of the bank's French customers. On this particular evening Mr. Lorry is sitting in his rooms at the bank. He glances out the window into the courtyard and sees a grindstone that has recently been placed there. Mr. Lorry shivers with a chill of foreboding and closes the blinds. The vague uneasiness that is upon him causes him to decide to go down to examine the bank to see if all is well, when suddenly the door opens and Lucie and Dr. Manette rush in. Mr. Lorry is overwhelmed, and in answer to his questions Lucie tells him that Charles came to Paris on a mission of mercy and has been taken and sent to prison. At the same moment is heard a loud noise of feet and voices in the courtyard. Dr. Manette goes to look but Mr. Lorry prevents him and rushes Lucie into the back room while he talks with her father. The two men go to the window and open the blind. In the courtyard are forty or fifty men and women gathered around the grindstone. Two men are working it and the rest are lined up to sharpen their weapons on it. All of the men and women are armed, with knives, swords, bayonets, axes, and all are soaked in blood. Blood is to be seen on the faces and the clothes of all assembled there, and as each finishes sharpening his weapon, he runs off into the street with a frenzied look in his eyes, gone mad with the lust for blood.

"They are murdering the prisoners," murmurs Mr. Lorry, and begs Dr. Manette to hurry down into the throng to attempt to rescue Charles Darnay before it is too late. Dr. Manette, as a former prisoner in the Bastille, has a certain power among the citizens of France and he is almost venerated because of his great suffering under the old régime. A moment later he appears in the courtyard and the crowd makes way for him. He speaks to them and they begin to cheer him. Mr. Lorry hears the words, "Save the prisoner Evrémonde at La Force," and sees the crowd, Dr. Manette in their widst, hurry out into the street. Mr. Lorry goes to Lucie to comfort her and to tell her tha her father has gone to save her husband. Lucie, under the great stress of the day, falls into a stupor, and Miss Pross and little Lucie, who have appeared, fall asleep on the bed. Twice more during the night, while Mr. Lorry sits watching over his charges, the bell at the gate sounds and a crowd rushes in to the grindstone and Lucie awakes with a start to be calmed again by Mr. Lorry. As the sun rises, Mr. Lorry looks out into the courtyard once again and sees the grindstone, covered with the red stain that will never be removed.

> **COMMENT:**   The swelling sea has now brought the rest of Charles Darnay's loved ones to Paris, as well as Miss Pross. Dr. Manette's new-found strength and power seems, for a moment, to be capable of obtaining Charles Darnay's release and, indeed, he will be successful in that undertaking. However, Mr. Lorry and Dr. Manette are not aware of the lengths to which the Defarges will go for vengeance, nor are they aware of Defarge's discovery in cell One Hundred and Five, North Tower, on the day that the Bastille fell. A brief moment of triumph for Dr. Manette will lead to redoubled anguish and pain when the discovery is revealed.

CHAPTER 3.   THE SHADOW

It occurs to Mr. Lorry, in his capacity as representative of Tellson's, that he should not imperil the operations of that banking institution by sheltering the wife of an emigrant prisoner under the same roof. At first he thinks of searching out Defarge and asking his advice on finding a safe dwelling for Lucie and her family while they are in Paris but, fortunately, he thinks better of that idea, realizing that the Saint Antoine district is the most violent quarter of Paris and Defarge is very likely deep in the dangerous workings of the Revolution there. Instead, with noon coming and the doctor not returning, Mr. Lorry goes out himself and finds a house nearby which he rents for Lucie and Dr. Manette, inasmuch as he has learned that Dr. Manette had planned on such a move himself. Mr. Lorry immediately moves Lucie and her child, and Miss Pross, to the house and leaves Jerry Cruncher with them to keep them safe.

In the evening, back in his room, Jarvis Lorry has a visitor. At first Mr. Lorry does not recognize him but it is Defarge. He has a message from Dr. Manette saying that Charles is safe and that the bearer of this message also has one for Lucie. He tells Mr. Lorry to take Defarge to her. Mr. Lorry and Defarge go out into the courtyard where they find two women waiting, one of them knitting. It is Madame Defarge whom Mr. Lorry recognizes in the same attitude as that in which he last saw her seventeen years ago; and with her is her companion known as The Vengeance. Madame Defarge is to go with the two men so that as Defarge explains, she will recognize those whom she has the power to protect should such protection become necessary. Mr. Lorry is slightly dubious about this and begins to be struck by Defarge's reserved and mechanical manner. They go to Lucie's lodgings and are admitted by Jerry Cruncher. They find Lucie alone, weeping. She is overjoyed to receive word from Charles and she reads the note raptly — "Dearest, — Take courage. I am well, and your father has influence around me. You cannot answer this. Kiss our child for me." Lucie, in her joy, grasps one of Madame Defarge's hands and kisses it, but the hand gives no response but only resumes its knitting. There is something about this impassive woman that terrifies Lucie, but Madame Defarge only looks at her with a cold state. Mr. Lorry breaks in to reassure Lucie, explaining that Madame Defarge is here to assure Lucie's safety, but he says this without conviction as he observes the stony manner of the three visitors. Miss Pross and little Lucie are called in, also to be recognized, and though Miss Pross is taken little heed of, Madame Defarge points her knitting needle at Little Lucie and speaks for the first time — "Is that his child?" Mr. Lorry answers yes. Lucie instinctively bends to hold the child to her heart as the shadow of Madame Defarge falls on little Lucie, so dark and threatening.

As the three prepare to go, Lucie grasps Madame Defarge's dress and begs for help. "You will be good to my poor husband. You will do him no harm. You will help me to see him if you can?" Madame Defarge looks down at her with perfect composure and replies, "Your husband is not my business here. It is the daughter of your father who is my business here . . . Surely the influence that your father has will release him." "As a wife and mother," cries Lucie earnestly, "I implore you to have pity on me and not to exercise any power that you possess, against my innocent husband, but to use it in his behalf." Madame Defarge, looking as cold as ever, turns to her friend The Vengeance and recalls that the women of France have for many years seen their husbands and fathers thrown into prison and all their lives they have seen their sisters and children suffer poverty, hunger, sickness, oppression. "Is it likely that the trouble of one wife and mother would be much to us now?" The three go out and Mr. Lorry tries to comfort Lucie, begging her to have a thankful heart, for things are going better with them now. "I am not thankless, I hope, but that dreadful woman seems to throw a shadow on me and on all my hopes." And despite his encouraging words, Mr. Lorry himself feels the shadow and is greatly troubled.

COMMENT: Lucie is cheered by the message from her husband but cast down again by the stoniness of her visitors. Madame Defarge has truly come to see them so that she may know them, but not for their protection. Her unfocused hatred for the family of the Marquis Saint Evrémonde has a focus now that she has seen Lucie and little Lucie, and Lucie's pleading carries no weight with her.

The vague shadow that Lucie feels cast over her will soon become more solid and real. Although Madame Defarge has taken little notice of Miss Pross, she will soon become acutely aware of her presence when the two women lock horns in combat over Lucie Darnay.

CHAPTER 4.   CALM IN STORM

On the fourth day since he went out into the courtyard, Dr. Manette returns. In the interim the prisons have been stormed and eleven hundred defenseless prisoners have been slain. Dr. Manette relates his experiences to Mr. Lorry. The crowd took him to La Force where he found a self-appointed tribunal sitting in judgment. The prisoners were brought before this tribunal and their fate quickly decided: they were either sent out to be massacred, were released, or, in a few cases, returned to their cells. Dr. Manette, having been presented to the tribunal and identified by Defarge, who was a member of the court, pleaded for his son-in-law's freedom and seemed on the verge of having his request granted when, after a hurried conference among the members of the tribunal, he was informed that Darnay could not be released but would be kept inviolate in safe custody. The doctor asked permission to remain there to make certain that Charles Darnay, through mischance or malice, was not turned over to the bloodthirsty crowd outside the prison. The permission was granted and Dr. Manette has remained there in the prison for three days until the danger passed. As Dr. Manette recounts all this to Mr. Lorry, the latter is struck by the strength and power which is evident in the doctor's demeanor. It is Dr. Manette's turn to be strong and restore his daughter's beloved husband to her, as she restored Dr. Manette to life. The years of suffering have been turned to good account and they are serving him in good stead in this new ordeal. Dr. Manette is finally appointed inspecting physician of three prisons, among them La Force, and is thus in a position to bring Lucie news of Charles. Darnay is no longer "in secret," but is confined with the other prisoners and Dr. Manette brings messages from him to Lucie each week. But try as he might, Dr. Manette is unable to secure Charles' release or even to get him brought to trial, for the tenor of the times is against it. The Revolution is still growing, the King and Queen have been beheaded and revolutionary tribunals have sprung up throughout France, ready to deliver innocent people into the sharp jaws of La Guillotine. In the midst of the terror, Dr. Manette walks with a steady tread, cautiously persistent, never doubting that he will save Lucie's husband. He stands as a man apart: silent, human, indispensable. But it has been one year and three months since Charles Darnay was imprisoned, and still there is no sign that he will be saved.

COMMENT: Dr. Manette's stature has grown and he has become a familiar figure in the prisons. But although it seemed at one moment that his powers were great enough to secure the release of his son-in-law, those hopes were quickly dashed. And although Darnay is still alive, he is still imprisoned and there is no certainty that he will not be beheaded the next morning. Through all this doubt and uncertainty and through the daily horrors which he sees, the doctor gains strength and his efforts will soon meet with success, albeit temporarily.

CHAPTER 5. THE WOOD-SAWYER

Ever since she moved into her new residence, Lucie has seen to it that the household has assumed a normal air; everything in its place, everything done at its appointed time. Little Lucie is taught by her mother regularly, as if they were at home. All is kept in readiness for Charles' homecoming. Such an approach to her situation helps to relieve Lucie's mind. Only at night, sometimes, does she lose her composure and weep on her father's breast, but he reassures her: "Nothing can happen to him without my knowledge, and I know that I can save him, Lucie."

One day, Dr. Manette returns home with the news that there is a certain window in the prison to which Charles can sometimes gain access at three in the afternoon. If Lucie were to stand at a certain spot, Charles could see her there, though she could not see him, and even if she could it would be unwise to give any sign of recognition. Thus, Lucie, the loving wife, begins to go out every day to stand in the appointed place so that her husband might get a glimpse of her. On the third day of her vigil, she is greeted by a cutter of wood whose house is nearby. He makes a gesture towards the prison to indicate that he knows why she is there. "But it's not my business," he mutters and goes on sawing wood. Lucie often meets him there, and sometimes, when she has forgotten herself and gazes up at the prison, she finds him looking at her. But he always mumbles the words, "But it's not my business," and falls to work again.

Months pass and, regardless of the weather, Lucie is at the spot each day. She hears from her father that only occasionally does Charles have the opportunity of seeing her, but on this small chance Lucie would wait out the day for her husband. As she is standing there one afternoon a crowd of people comes around the corner of the prison. Among them can be seen the wood-sawyer, and as she watches, the crowd begins to dance the Carmagnole, the grotesque, devilish dance which has been spawned by the Revolution, a dance in which blood is angered, senses bewildered, and hearts steeled for the orgy of bloodletting which often follows it. They surround her, dancing wildly, until finally they pass and leave Lucie behind, frightened and bewildered, as her father appears. He comforts her and tells her that, as there is no one about, she may blow a kiss in the direction of the prison window. She does so and suddenly Madame Defarge is there. She and Dr. Manette exchange a greeting and she is gone. Nothing more.

Dr. Manette tells Lucie that Charles is to be summoned before the tribunal the next day and that he, Dr. Manette, must make certain final preparations before then; in doing so, he must see Mr. Lorry. As Lucie and her father stand in the street, three tumbrils (carts) pass filled with their human cargo bound for the Guillotine. When Lucie and Dr. Manette reach the bank, Mr. Lorry comes out to them, agitated, and there is a coat on the chair belonging to some visitor. Mr. Lorry turns to the room he has just left as he repeats Lucie's words: "Summoned for tomorrow?"

> **COMMENT:** The wood-sawyer whom we met in this chapter is none other than the former mender of roads whom we have seen earlier. His casual remarks are not so casual as they seem and the appearance of Madame Defarge on the scene, in time to see Lucie's greeting to her husband, indicates that the wood-sawyer has told his tale to her. She duly makes a note of the fact and goes' her way. The unknown visitor at Mr. Lorry's is Sydney Carton who has made his entry onto the stage in this last act of the drama and who will leave it in another role. His arrival sets the scene for the "hand of cards" we mentioned earlier and the playing of the trump card by Jerry Cruncher.

CHAPTER 6.   TRIUMPH

The day dawns and the dread tribunal of five judges, Public Prosecutor, and Jury sits, as it sits every day. The list is read and there are twenty-three names called before the Tribunal today. Only twenty appear, however, for two have died in jail and one has already been guillotined and forgotten. Charles Darnay is the sixteenth to appear. Of the fifteen before him, all have been condemned in the space of only an hour and a half. As Charles Darnay takes his place before the court, he sees the Defarges sitting in the front row but they look only at the jury, never glancing his way.

Near the President of the Tribunal sits Dr. Manette. The hearing gets under way. It is stated by the prosecutor that Darnay is an emigrant and, under the existing decree, all emigrants who return to France are doomed to death. It matters not that the decree has been passed since Darnay's return. "Take off his head," cries the crowd. The President of the Tribunal then questions Darnay and it is revealed that Darnay has relinquished a title distasteful to him and left France to live by his own industry in England, rather than on the industry of the downtrodden people of France. In proof of this, Darnay submits the names of two witnesses: Gabelle and Dr. Manette. But, the President reminds him, he has married in England. True, but not an Englishwoman. A citizeness of France? Yes, by birth. Her name and family? "Lucie Manette, only daughter of Doctor Manette, the good physician who sits there." This reply has an electric effect on the audience, and the very same people who a moment ago were clamoring for Darnay's death, now weep with sympathy.

Gabelle is then called and he testifies to the truth of Darnay's statement that he came back to save Gabelle's life. Then Dr. Manette is questioned. His popularity and his careful answers make a great impression. He testifies to Darnay's friendship and devotion to himself and to his daughter, that, far from being a friend of the aristocracy in England, he had actually been tried as an enemy by it, for being friendly toward the United States. The jury interrupts the testimony, saying that they have heard enough. The jury then votes, singly and aloud, and the populace sets up a shout of applause. All the members of the jury are in Darnay's favor and the President declares him free.

Darnay is overwhelmed by the throng of well-wishers determined to embrace him, these same people who, if the verdict had been different, would have torn him to pieces. As he and Dr. Manette leave the court, the crowd surrounds them, weeping and embracing. It seems to Darnay that everyone who was at the hearing is now on the streets surrounding him. Only two faces are missing — Monsieur and Madame Defarge. The crowd carries Darnay home on their shoulders, while Dr. Manette goes on ahead to inform Lucie. Finally, husband and wife are united and the crowd breaks into the Carmagnole and dances away. As the family is reunited and everyone greets Charles Darnay, he says to Lucie, "And now speak to your father, dearest. No other man in France could have done what he has done for me." And as Lucie lays her head on her father's breast, he is repaid for his sufferings and proud of his strength. "You must not be weak, my darling. Don't tremble so. I have saved him."

COMMENT: At last Charles Darnay has been summoned before the Tribunal. The months of anguish awaiting this day are over and he is finally permitted to testify. Dr. Manette's careful instructions concerning his testimony have borne fruit and from the first words the crowd has been with him and he has been set free, to the great joy of all except the Defarges. But they are not done with Charles Darnay; his freedom will be short-lived. In a few hours time he will once again be imprisoned, this time not accused under a revolutionary decree, but accused directly by three citizens of France: Monsieur and Madame Defarge and one other. And the testimony of this one other, though given-second-hand and unwillingly, will prove to be the most damning testimony imaginable and will seal Charles Darnay's doom.

CHAPTER 7. A KNOCK AT THE DOOR

Glad as she is to have her husband returned to her, Lucie's heart is not at ease. Every day men and women as innocent as her husband have been fed to the ravenous guillotine, and revenge and hate hang so heavy in the air that fear is always with her for her husband's safety. Dr. Manette, now supremely confident because of the strength he has shown in effecting Charles' release, makes light of Lucie's fears. Both because of their straitened circumstances and the fact that it is wise not to show any conspicuous wealth which would offend the populace, the Darnay's keep no servants. Jerry Cruncher, who has been transferred to the Darnay household by Mr. Lorry, and Miss Pross, do all the shopping for the house. Each afternoon they set forth, Miss Pross with the money, Jerry with a basket, for the market where they make their careful purchases. Inasmuch as it is still dangerous to leave Paris, the household routine goes on as usual.

On this particular afternoon Jerry and Miss Pross set out on their accustomed outing leaving Lucie, Charles, and Dr. Manette at home. Dr. Manette is telling his granddaughter a story. Suddenly Lucie shouts, "What's that?" Her father tries to calm her, but she insists that she heard footsteps on the stairs. "My love, the staircase is as still as Death." As Dr. Manette speaks the word a knock is heard at the door. Lucie is beside herself with fear as Dr. Manette goes to the door and opens it. Four rough men, all armed and wearing the red caps of the Jacquerie, enter. They have come for Charles Darnay who is to be summoned again before the Tribunal tomorrow. Dr. Manette is as if turned to stone. His questions are hesitantly answered and finally it is learned that the Defarges — and one other — have denounced Darnay. When Dr. Manette asks the identity of the "one other," the man from St. Antoine gives him a strange look but does not answer the question. Thus, Charles Darnay, recently released, is once again returned to prison.

COMMENT: Their care not to attract attention and to remain as inconspicuous as possible comes to nought. The Furies (the ancient Greek goddesses of revenge) have searched out their victim, and though he temporarily escaped their clutches, they have once again fastened their claws into his flesh and will not let him get away so easily this time. We are about to have the loose threads of this narrative brought together — the details of Dr. Manette's imprisonment, the history of Charles Darnay's family, the reason for Madame Defarge's undying hatred for the name Evrémonde and all who bear it. And when we know all these things, Charles Darnay's future will seem quite hopeless. And indeed it is, save for a verbal hand at cards to be played by three men: Sydney Carton, John Barsad, and Jerry Cruncher.

CHAPTER 8.   A HAND AT CARDS

Jerry Cruncher and Miss Pross are threading their way to the market-place, unaware of the calamity that has just taken place at home. Having made a few small purchases, Miss Pross remembers that they must buy some wine. They go to a shop nearby which seems quieter than most. There are a number of people in the wine shop in various attitudes — drinking, smoking, playing dominos, reading a newspaper. Our two friends go to the counter and tell the man there what they want. A man rises from a table in the corner and starts toward the door. In so doing he comes face to face with Miss Pross who takes one look at him, screams, and claps her hands. The crowd is on its feet in a moment, expecting that someone has been murdered. The man mutters a few words to Miss Pross in English in a vexed, abrupt voice. "Oh Solomon, dear Solomon!" cries Miss Pross, deeply affected by seeing her brother again under such circumstances. "Don't call me Solomon. Do you want to be the death of me?" the man says in a frightened way. He tells Miss Pross to pay for the wine and come outside if she wishes to speak with him. With a few words in French the man calms the spectators who all fall back into their former places and pursuits. The three go outside to continue their conversation. All this time Jerry Cruncher has been silent and staring as if he had seen a ghost.

> **COMMENT:**   In a manner of speaking, he has, for the man had another identity when Jerry, and we, first saw him.

It is clear that Solomon is not at all happy to have been seen by Miss Pross, and he tries to get her to go away and not endanger his life by her chatter, but Miss Pross asks only for a kind, friendly word from this brother who, long ago, stole her money and left her behind. At this point Jerry Cruncher speaks up for the first time. Hs asks Solomon whether his name is John Solomon or Solomon John. Solomon eyes him suspiciously. "Come!" says Mr. Cruncher, "John Solomon, or Solomon John? She calls you Solomon, and she must know, being your sister. And *I* know you're John, you know. Which of the two goes first? And regarding that name of Pross, likewise. That warn't your name over the water." Solomon plays dumb and Jerry, though he remembers that the other's name over the water had two syllables, cannot, for the life of him, think what it was. "Barsad," comes the answer, from a new voice that has joined the conversation.

> **COMMENT:**   John Barsad, the chief witness against Charles Dar-nay in the spy trial in England, former spy for the French mon-archy, and now serving as an "official" for the Revolutionary gov-ernment. The speaker who reveals the man's identity is Sydney

Carton who arrived in Paris the evening before. Only Mr. Lorry, to this moment, knew of Carton's presence, but the time has come for him to reveal himself and to proceed with the course of action that is beginning to form in his mind.

John Barsad, or Solomon Pross, is employed as a "sheep of the prisons," that is, a spy for the jailers, an unsavory occupation in keeping with his unsavory past in England. Carton asks Barsad to join him at Tellson's Bank for a few minutes of conversation. The request is spoken lightly, but there is a vague threat in the words and the spy catches the implication and agrees to go with Carton. They see Miss Pross home and then the three men, Barsad, Carton, and Jerry Cruncher proceed to Mr. Lorry's rooms. Carton introduces the spy to Mr. Lorry who looks at him with undisguised abhorrence, and then he informs Mr. Lorry that Charles Darnay has been rearrested. Mr. Lorry is struck dumb by the news but the determination in Carton's face tells him that it is no use to talk about it further.

Carton, at this point, announces that the desperateness of the situation requires that he win a friend in the prison and the friend he intends to win is none other than John Barsad. "You need have good cards, sir," answers the spy. "I'll run them over. I'll see what I hold," answers Carton as he pours himself some brandy. Carton's cards are these: Barsad, a spy and secret informer who represents himself to his employers under a false name; Barsad, who is now employed by the republican French government was formerly employed by the aristocratic English government, the enemy of France and of freedom, the inference being that Barsad is still working as a spy for the English and has worked his way into the French Republic for the benefit of England. Barsad grows uneasy and Carton then plays his ace: denunciation of Barsad to the nearest Citizen's Committee which will shortly cause him to be added to the list of the guillotine's victims. "Look over your hand, Mr. Barsad, and see what you have. Don't hurry." Barsad grows more fearful as he sees Carton down brandy after brandy, thinking that he might drink himself into such a state that he might denounce him immediately.

Barsad considers his hand. It is not a good one. It is even worse than Carton suspects. For, besides serving as a spy for the British, he also served as a spy for the French aristocratic government and it was in this role that he appeared at Defarge's wine-shop. He knows that Madame Defarge has registered him in her knitting and that she has already denounced many whose names were woven in that register. He knows that with that terrible woman his life is never safe. Barsad is overwhelmed and at a loss. He sees that he is at Carton's mercy. And then Carton recalls that he has another card that he has not yet played. Carton has observed Barsad with another sheep of the prison whom he believes he recognized. The light dawns. "Cly! Disguised, but the same man. We had that same man before us at the Old Bailey." Barsad resumes his confident air. No, Carton is mistaken, for Cly has been dead several years and was buried in London. Barsad even has the death certificate to prove it.

At this point an unusual thing happens. Jerry Cruncher, whose hair is standing straight up, steps forward, touches Barsad's shoulder, and speaks — "That there Roger Cly, master. So *you* put him in his coffin?" "I did," answers Barsad. "Who took him out of it?" asks Jerry. The spy stammers, "What do you mean?" "I mean," continues Jerry, "that he warn't never in it . . . I tell you that you buried paving-stones and earth in that there coffin. Don't go and tell *me* that you buried Cly. It was a take in. Me and two more knows it." All three men are speechless with astonishment at this turn of events. "I see one thing," says Carton. "I hold another card, Mr. Barsad . . . You are in communication with another aristocratic spy of the same antecedents as yourself, who, moreover, has the mystery about him of having feigned death and come to life again! A strong card — a certain Guillotine card! Do you play?" It is too much for Barsad and he gives up. Carton takes him into the other room to make his proposition known to the spy.

> COMMENT: Jerry Cruncher's nocturnal wanderings have provided Sydney Carton with the final lever he needs to get Barsad to do his bidding. Barsad warns that an escape is impossible but Carton says that he has never suggested such a plan. His scheme is much more bold and devious, a scheme whose daring seems to hold little chance of success. But it is destined to be carried out nevertheless, and in accomplishing it Sydney Carton is to achieve a stature not conceivable for him before this time.

CHAPTER 9. THE GAME MADE

While Carton and Barsad are conferring in the next room, Mr. Lorry looks at Jerry Cruncher with considerable doubt and mistrust. Mr. Lorry tells Jerry that if has practiced an unlawful occupation, as the evidence seems to show he has, then he is not to expect that Mr. Lorry will keep his secret from Tellson's when they return to England. But Jerry, in a long and involved speech, persuades Mr. Lorry of his good intentions and promises to reform when they return home. Mr. Lorry relents and drops the subject.

Carton and Barsad then come out and Barsad leaves. Mr. Lorry asks Carton what he has done. "Not much. If it should go ill with the prisoner, I have ensured access to him, once." Mr. Lorry's face falls at the seeming inadequacy of this arrangement. "It is all I could do," continues Carton, "there is no help for it." Carton asks that his presence not be made known to Lucie and that she not be told of the arrangements concerning Darnay. Sydney Carton and Mr. Lorry then chat about Mr. Lorry's long years of service and his reward of love and respect from those who know him. It is clear that Carton's years are a curse to him, for he has achieved nothing and no one cares for him. Mr. Lorry has never seen the man so open and gentle and he gives him his hand warmly. Carton sees Mr. Lorry to the Darnay house and takes leave of him, telling him that he, too, will be in court on the morrow.

Carton meets the wood-sawyer and passes a few words with him. The man obviously takes great delight in watching the executioner at work. We learn, in passing, that Carton is so versed in French that he speaks the language like a true Frenchman.

> **COMMENT:**　An important point. It is essential for Carton to be more French than Darnay himself in the role that he is about to play.

Carton walks on and stops at a chemist's shop where he purchases two packets of certain chemicals. The chemist warns him to keep the two separate because of their effect when mixed. Carton takes the packets and goes out. He wanders through the city, for he knows that he will not sleep this night. He carries a little girl across a muddy street and he sees the sun rise. He falls asleep on the bank of a stream. Then he awakes, returns to Mr. Lorry's to refresh himself, and sets out for the trial.

From his obscure corner at the court, Sydney Carton can see Mr. Lorry and Dr. Manette and Lucie. The same determined patriots are on the jury, prominent among them a man with a craving on his face — a life-thirsting, bloody-minded juryman, the Jacques Three of Saint Antoine. There is a murderous feeling apparent among the Prosecutor and five Judges today, not the favorable leaning of Darnay's earlier hearing. The hearing begins. The accused is openly denounced. By whom? "Three voices. Ernest Defarge, wine vendor of Saint Antoine. Therese Defarge, his wife. And Alexandre Manette, physician. A great uproar follows the reading of Dr. Manette's name. That good doctor rises to deny any accusations by him, but the President of the Tribunal silences him.

Defarge is called and recounts his former life in the service of Dr. Manette, the occasion of the imprisonment, the Doctor's later release and his own part in tending to the doctor after his release. The Vengeance interrupts the hearing with praise for Defarge's part in the taking of the Bastille. The crowd is clearly with him. Defarge continues his story: On the day the Bastille fell he proceeded to the cell where Dr. Manette had formerly been imprisoned, and in searching it found a scrap of paper, the handwriting on which proved to be Dr. Manette's. Defarge presents the paper to the President of the Tribunal and the order is given that it be read.

COMMENT: The die is cast. Sydney Carton has made his arrangements with John Barsad, and although to Mr. Lorry they seem painfully inadequate, they fully serve Carton's plans. Once again, in his conversation with Mr. Lorry, Sydney Carton reveals his deep love and admiration for Lucie Darnay and sets the scheme in motion that will make good his promise to her, that he would die to save anyone she loved. At Darnay's second trial we learn the name of Darnay's third accuser: none other than Dr. Manette himself. And though the doctor protests at this, the document he wrote so long ago in his prison cell is produced and the reading of it will make clear that Dr. Manette *does* accuse Charles Darnay and even damns him, albeit in the name of his family, for, of course, he had no acquaintance with Darnay himself at that time. In the next chapter we are to learn all the missing facts about the imprisonment and its consequences.

CHAPTER 10. THE SUBSTANCE OF THE SHADOW

And so Dr. Manette's old diary is read. The diary was written with a rusty iron point dipped in scrapings of soot and charcoal mixed with blood, written in great secrecy and hidden away in the chimney. ——— On a cloudy December night in 1757, the doctor was walking by the Seine when a carriage pulled up near him. Someone called his name. He answered and two men got out of the carriage and came up to him. They assured themselves that he was the Doctor Manette they were seeking. They then asked him, in a peremptory manner, to enter the carriage. He had no choice but to do so. The carriage sped off with its three passengers and finally stopped at a solitary house. After opening a gate to let them in, one of the men locked it behind them. As they entered the house, the doctor noticed that the two men were twin brothers.

From the time that they had left the carriage, Dr. Manette had noticed cries from a room on an upper floor. The doctor was led to this chamber and discovered that his patient was a beautiful young woman in great mental turmoil, lying on a bed, her arms bound to her sides with a gentleman's scarf bearing armorial devices and the letter E. She would utter piercing shrieks, repeat the words, "My husband, my father, and my brother!" count up to twelve and say, "Hush!" There would be a moment's pause and then the shrieks, and the process would begin over again. The two brothers stood by while Dr. Manette examined the girl, and they answered his questions in a short, haughty manner. After he had administered a sedative, provided by the brothers, he was told that there was another patient. Surprised, the Doctor followed the brothers and in a nearby room there lay a young peasant boy, no more than seventeen, mortally wounded by a sword-thrust. It was clear that he

could not live much longer. When Dr. Manette asked the elder brother
how this had happened (Dr. Manette used the term "elder brother" to
indicate the one who seemed to be in authority), the reply was, "A
crazed young common dog! a serf! Forced my brother to draw upon
him, and has fallen by my brother's sword — like a gentleman." There
was no pity in the voice but only disgust that a gentleman had had to
deal with a mere peasant, and annoyance that such a one had to die
there, so inconveniently.

The boy, with his last ounce of strength, raised himself up to tell his
story to Dr. Manette. His family were poor peasants and they were
miserably oppressed by the two brothers as peasants were oppressed
throughout France by the nobility. His sister had married a man of her
class, a man who was ill and whom she cared for and tended. The
younger of the two brothers happened to see her one day and was at-
tracted to her. He asked his brother, who bore the title of Marquis and
controlled the land, to lend her to him. The Marquis was agreeable, for
it was the prerogative of the nobles to help themselves to any peasant
women who struck their fancy. But the virtuous girl refused and bore
great hatred for the younger brother. They then began working her
husband day and night so that he might persuade his wife to surrender
to the younger brother. But he did not give in and one day, at noon, he
sobbed twelve times, once for every stroke of the bell, and died on his
wife's bosom. The wife was then taken away by the two brothers for the
pleasure of the younger. When her father learned of her fate, his heart
burst. The girl's brother had then hidden away his younger sister to
save her from a similar fate, and had climbed into the house where he
challenged the younger brother who had been forced to unsheath his
sword and mortally wound him. Then, after telling his story to Dr.
Manette, the young boy uttered a curse on the two brothers and on all
their race, and fell back, dead.

The doctor returned to the girl who was still shrieking and repeating
the same words. At last she sank into a lethargy and Dr. Manette, in
composing her as she lay on the bed, discovered that she was with child
and he lost all hope for her. She lingered for a week, then she died
without revealing her family name, exactly as her brother had done.
Upon learning the news of her death, the Marquis turned to his brother
and said, "I congratulate you, my brother." They then offered Dr. Manette a gold coin which he refused and warned him that all that he had
seen and heard was to remain a secret. They left without another word
and Dr. Manette was driven home.

The next morning he found the gold coin in a box at his door. Dr.
Manette decided to write a letter to the Court Minister telling the details of the affair, in order to ease his mind, although he was quite aware
of the immunity of the nobles and suspected that nothing would come

of it. Accordingly, he wrote the letter, without mentioning names, and later delivered it himself. After he had finished it, he was told a lady was waiting to see him. She identified herself as the wife of the Marquis Saint Evrémonde, the elder brother. She knew the story of that fateful night when the doctor was summoned and wished somehow to make whatever amends she could. She asked Dr. Manette if he knew the address of the younger sister so that she might do something for her but, unhappily, he did not. She was a good, compassionate lady, unhappily married, but determined to do what she could. As the doctor saw her to the door, there was a young boy waiting in the carriage for his mother. It was for his sake, she told the doctor, that she wished to make amends for the sins of the Saint Evrémonde family, for she continued, "I have a presentiment that if no other innocent atonement is made for this, it will one day be required of him." She then drove off.

That evening, a man in dark dress rang at the doctor's gate, was admitted by the doctor's servant, Ernest Defarge, and he informed the doctor that there was an urgent case that required his attention. When Dr. Manette left the house, he was bound and gagged. The two brothers then stepped out of the darkness, and identified him with a gesture. The Marquis then held the doctor's letter before him and burnt it with the flame of a lantern. Not a word was spoken. Doctor Manette was then brought to his cell, One Hundred and Five, North Tower, where he remained buried for eighteen years. Dr. Manette closed his document with the words, "And them and their descendants, to the last of their race, I, Alexandre Manette, unhappy prisoner, do this last night of the year 1767, in my unbearable agony, denounce to the times when all these things shall be answered for. I denounce them to Heaven and to earth."

As this narrative is finished being read, a bloodthirsty sound arises from the court. At every juryman's vote, there is a roar. Another and another. Unanimously voted. Death for the accused within four-and-twenty hours! Madame Defarge, smiling, turns to The Vengeance and speaks. "Much influence around him, has that doctor? Save him now, my Doctor, save him!"

COMMENT: At last the story is known, the story of that awful night many years ago when darkness fell over Dr. Manette. A pair of decadent noblemen, the father and uncle of Charles Darnay, used to helping themselves to what they want, steal a peasant girl after tormenting her husband to death. The Marquis, Darnay's father, aids his brother in this plan, for it is the uncle who wishes the girl. Suddenly, the uncle is confronted by the girl's avenging brother and is forced to draw his sword to defend himself. Dr. Manette, a young, rising physician in Paris, is called upon to minister to these dying wretches, brother and sister. He later meets the wife of the Marquis, a decent woman, and catches a glimpse of the young Charles Darnay, her son. The mother prophetically mentions that unless she makes amends herself for the crimes of the family Charles will one day be called upon to pay for the sins of his father and uncle. The good doctor, to ease his conscience, writes a letter to the minister, but the nobility is invulnerable and for his pains he is taken from his home and cast into prison, never to be accused, never to offer testimony, while the two brothers live to pursue their evil ways. The reading of this document to the crowded court has the effect desired by the Defarges who have been holding the document, biding their time until the opportune moment. The sentence is death for Charles Darnay, fulfilling his mother's premonitions that his life would be forfeit unless she found the dead girl's sister in order to help her. But because she was not found Madame Defarge gloats over her victory. We shall soon learn why these two results have a connection with one another.

CHAPTER 11. DUSK

As the court empties Lucie and Charles join in a last embrace before he is returned to his cell for the last time. Dr. Manette is mad with anguish but Darnay soothes him, saying, "We know now what you underwent when you suspected my descent, and when you knew it . . . It could not be otherwise. All things have worked together as they have fallen out . . . Be comforted and forgive me." As he is led away, Lucie faints and Sydney Carton steps up and carries her to a waiting carriage. He, Lucie, Mr. Lorry, and Dr. Manette proceed to Lucie's lodgings where Carton carries her up to her room tenderly. He bends over, kisses her cheek and whispers something. Little Lucie many years later is to reveal his words: "A life you love." Carton, before he goes, begs Dr. Manette to intercede once more with the officials although there is little hope in the present situation. Dr. Manette assures Carton that he shall, and will know the results by dark. Carton says that he will come by Mr. Lorry's at nine to learn of them. As Mr. Lorry sees Carton to the door he says, "But he will perish; there is no real hope." "Yes, He will perish; there is no real hope," repeats Carton and walks out with a settled air about him.

COMMENT: Sydney Carton now sees that the time has come to set his plan into motion. After seeing Lucie safely home, he asks Dr. Manette to try once again to save Darnay, not really expecting any good to come of it, but wishing Lucie to feel that everything that could have been done was done. His reason for checking back in the evening is to make certain that there is no hope for Darnay before he commits himself to the scheme from which there is no turning back.

CHAPTER 12. DARKNESS

Sydney Carton pauses in the street, not certain what he should do while waiting until the nine o'clock meeting. He decides that it is best to show himself, and after dinner and a nap he proceeds to Defarge's wine-shop. The Defarges, Jacques Three, and The Vengeance are the only people in the shop as he enters. He orders a glass of wine in fumbling French and Madame Defarge is quick to perceive the physical resemblance between him and Darnay. He pretends to have difficulty with the French language as the Defarges bid him Good Evening and he sits down at a table to study a French newspaper. They grow careless because of his seeming lack of knowledge of French and so they do not attempt to cover their conversation. Carton, pretending to be absorbed in his newspaper, hears that Madame Defarge wishes to destroy Dr. Manette, Lucie and little Lucie, as well as Darnay. Defarge, remembering his years as a servant of Dr. Manette and the compassion of Lucie for her husband, demurs, and wishes them to be spared. But Madame Defarge is like stone and she is commended by Jacques Three and The Vengeance for her zeal. We then learn the reason for Madame Defarge's unending hatred for the Evrémonde family: *She* was the sister who was hidden away by the boy before he crossed swords with the brother of the Marquis. The dead sister and brother were *her* sister and brother and she will stop at nothing to wipe out all traces of her family of Evrémonde to avenge her own family. "Then tell Wind and Fire where to stop but don't tell me," she says. Defarge can do nothing but give in to her wishes.

Carton pays for his wine and goes out. At nine o'clock he appears at Mr. Lorry's. Jarvis Lorry is in a state of agitation — Dr. Manette has not come back. At ten he goes out to see about Lucie while Carton waits for the doctor. At twelve Mr. Lorry returns and still no sign of Dr. Manette. Then they hear him on the stairs. As he enters they see that all is lost. "Where is my bench? What have they done with my work? Time presses: I must finish those shoes." Lost, utterly lost! They calm him and persuade him to sit down by the fire and his work will be brought presently. It is then that Sydney Carton reveals to Mr. Lorry what his part will be in the scheme devised to save Lucie and Dr. Manette. Mr. Lorry has already made arrangements to leave France. Carton removes a paper from the Doctor's wallet: it is a pass out of Paris for Dr. Manette, Lucie and little Lucie. He gives this to Mr. Lorry along with his own pass and instructs Mr. Lorry to keep the papers safe and to make everything ready for a departure the next afternoon, for he has heard from Madame Defarge's own lips that she will stop at nothing to sawyer in his testimony that he has seen Lucie signaling to the prisoner.

exterminate the whole family and she has already rehearsed the wood—
Mr. Lorry catches the flame of Carton's manner and listens to him attentively, promising that all will be arranged. He learns from Carton that they are all to be in the coach the next afternoon and when he, Carton, arrives to occupy his place in the coach, they are to make for England as quickly as possible. After seeing Dr. Manette home, Carton bids goodbye to Mr. Lorry and breathes a farewell to Lucie as he looks up at her lighted room.

> **COMMENT:** All is made ready for the daring plan of Carton's. The success of it now depends on himself, on Mr. Lorry, and on John Barsad, who has access to the prisons. In his new-found certainty of purpose, Sydney Carton is carrying out his promise to Lucie to lay down his life for one she holds dear. Once again the resemblance between him and Charles Darnay is to save Darnay's life, but things must be done swiftly for Madame Defarge's hatred is seething and in a short while will reach out for Charles Darnay's family. And this hatred, in so doing, will swallow up Madame Defarge herself and spare her would-be victims.

CHAPTER 13. FIFTY-TWO

In the black prison of the Conciergerie, fifty-two doomed prisoners await their execution on this day. One of them is Charles Darnay. Alone, in his cell, he has calmed himself and assumed an air of resolution. He writes a tender letter to Lucie telling her of his promise to her father and of his own ignorance of the role his family had played in the doctor's imprisonment, and begging her to comfort her father in his anguish. He also writes a letter to Dr. Manette, confiding his wife and child to his care, and a letter to Mr. Lorry, settling his business affairs. His mind never thinks of the man who is about to die for him — Sydney Carton.

Shortly after one o'clock, footsteps are heard and Sydney Carton is let into Darnay's cell. Darnay is dombfounded. "You are not a prisoner?" "No, I come from her — your wife, dear Darnay." Carton quickly commands Darnay to change clothes with him. The bewildered Darnay complies, but doubtfully. "Carton, there is no escaping from this place; it never can be done. You will only die with me. It is madness." Carton ignores these comments and orders Darnay to sit and write as he dictates; Darnay does so. "If you remember the words that passed between us, long ago, you will readily comprehend this when you see it. I am thankful that the time has come, when I can prove them. That I do so is no subject for regret or grief." As Carton speaks, he removes his hand from his coat and brings it close to Darnay's face. The drug that he purchased earlier takes effect. Darnay's hand trails off and in a moment

Carton's hand is over Darnay's face, his arm around his waist. The struggle lasts but a moment: Darnay lies insensible on the floor. Carton puts the paper in Darnay's coat, calls to Barsad, and orders him to take Darnay out. On the way into the prison Carton had pretended to be weak and faint in order to prepare the guard for the condition of the man Barsad is to lead out. "You swear not to betray me?" murmurs the trembling spy. "Your life is in your own hand. Quick, call assistance," answers Carton. He tells the spy to take Darnay to the waiting coach and to remind Mr. Lorry of his promise. Barsad calls two gaolers and they take Darnay out, unconscious. The door closes behind them and Carton listens for the sound of an alarm, but there is none.

A short while later, "Evrémonde" is called and he and his fifty-one fellow prisoners are assembled in a large, dark room. As he waits, a young seamstress comes up to him who was imprisoned with Darnay in La Force. She talks with him, asks to ride with him in the tumbril, and then a doubt crosses her face. The deception is discovered! But she whispers, "Are you dying for him?" "And his wife and child?" "Hush! Yes." "O you will let me hold your brave hand, stranger?" "Hush! Yes, my poor sister; to the last."

At the same moment, a coach reaches the outskirts of Paris and a guard demands the papers of its occupants. Mr. Lorry identifies each: Dr. Manette, Lucie, little Lucie, "Sydney Carton," and himself. The coach is permitted to go on; the first danger passed! Lucie is anxious about pursuit but the road behind is clear. At a posting-house their horses are changed and a citizen calls to them. Are they discovered? But no; he wishes simply to learn the number of those condemned today. The coach once again is under way and soon will reach the Channel and safety.

COMMENT: The scheme has worked. With the aid of Barsad, Sydney Carton has gained admittance to the cell of Charles Darnay. He has changed clothes with him, drugged him, and has had him dragged out by Barsad to the waiting coach. The coach is on its way to safety, and, except for a brief moment of uncertainty, Carton is accepted as Evrémonde and will soon ride the tumbril to his death. Barring a last-minute discovery, the plan has succeeded completely. And, barring a last-minute discovery by Madame Defarge, the five passengers in the coach are safe. But even now she is planning to take the lives of Lucie and her child. Only Miss Pross and Jerry Cruncher remain behind to cover the tracks, and now the determined Frenchwoman and the equally determined Englishwoman are to meet once again and are to do battle to the death.

CHAPTER 14. THE KNITTING DONE

Madame Defarge meets with Jacques Three and The Vengeance, not at the wine-shop but at the shed of the wood-sawyer. Madame Defarge speaks: "My husband is a good Republican and a bold man; but he has his weaknesses and he is so weak as to relent towards this doctor. I care nothing nothing for this doctor, I: He may wear his head or lose it. But, the Evrémonde people are to be exterminated, and the wife and child must follow the husband and father." Her companions agree eagerly. But then she changes her mind and decides that Dr. Manette must die, too. After the day's executions they are to meet in Saint Antoine and the wood-sawyer will testify against Lucie and her father. Madame Defarge decides to go to visit Lucie, for undoubtedly she will utter something against the Republic in despair at losing her husband and this will provide additional evidence. Madame Defarge gives her knitting to The Vengeance, tells her to save a chair at the executions, and goes out to Lucie's lodgings. She walks with a confident tread, a dagger and pistol in her clothing, overwhelming hatred in her heart.

Meanwhile, Miss Pross and Jerry Cruncher are preparing their own departure. Mr. Lorry has arranged for them to leave later, in a lighter carriage, so that the first coach won't be slowed down and so that, in the lighter carriage, Jerry and Miss Pross will overtake the first and can make arrangements for fresh horses at stopping places to expedite the escape and save precious time. In the midst of this preparation, Jerry Cruncher vows that he will never do it again (referring to his grave robbing), and will henceforth permit Mrs. Cruncher to "flop" all she pleases. And all the while Madame Defarge draws nearer.

It is agreed that Jerry wil get the coach and Miss Pross will meet him elsewhere so as not to arouse suspicion with two coaches leaving from the same place. Jerry goes out to make the arrangements and Miss Pross begins to get herself ready for the trip. Suddenly she looks up and cries out. There stands Madame Defarge. Neither speaks the other's language, but it is clear to both that they are diametrically opposed in their intentions — one to save the family, the other to destroy it. Miss Pross realizes that the open doors will suggest flight to Madame Defarge, so she closes them and takes up her position in front of Lucie's chamber. Madame Defarge demands to see Lucie and Miss Pross refuses to let her. The words are not understood but the meaning of each woman is clear to the other. Something tells Madame Defarge that her quarry has flown and she opens three of the doors; all is in disorder. But she must make certain. She once again demands that Miss Pross let her look in the room before which she stands. Miss Pross refuses. Madame Defarge makes for the door and the two women struggle. Madame Defarge reaches for her pistol; Miss Pross sees it and strikes at it. The gun goes off. And the lifeless body of Madame Defarge falls to the floor.

Miss Pross puts on her bonnet, locks the door behind her, and, after taking a moment to breathe and to cry, rushes out to meet Jerry. Her face is scratched and her hair torn but fortunately her veil hides most of this evidence. She meets Jerry at the cathedral and they drive away. As they ride along the streets of Paris, the awful rumble of the carts taking the fifty-two condemned souls to the guillotine can be heard. But not by Miss Pross. For the exploding pistol has deafened her, and she is never to hear anything again.

> **COMMENT:** The last obstacle has been cleared away with the death of Madame Defarge who has been consumed by her hatred and slain by her own hand. Nothing can prevent the two coaches of people from reaching England and safety. And even now the tumbrils are drawing near to the place of execution, bearing Sydney Carton, alias the Marquis Saint Evrémonde, to his final reward.

CHAPTER 15. THE FOOTSTEPS DIE OUT FOREVER

Six tumbrils carry the day's victims to La Guillotine. The condemned stand silent, some observing the people in the streets, some sunk in silent despair. There is great curiosity among the people to see the aristocrat Evrémonde. When he is pointed out, he is seen standing in the third tumbril with the head bent down, talking to a young girl. The carts reach their destinetion. In front of the guillotine are a number of chairs occupied by women, knitting. Among them is The Vengeance. "Therese. Who has seen her? Therese Defarge!" she cries. But Madame Defarge cannot hear her, and as the tumbrils begin to empty and the heads begin to fall, the knitting women count. One! Two! As the crowd of victims begins to thin out, the little seamstress, who has been holding Carton's head for comfort, thanks him for his kindness and then it is her turn. She kisses Carton and mounts the scaffold. The blade falls: Twenty-Two. And then Sydney Carton's turn is come. Twenty-Three. And it is over.

It is said about the city that the man Evrémonde had the most peaceful look on his face that had ever been seen. If he had been able to write his last thoughts before he died, they would have been something like this: I see a beautiful city and a brilliant people rising from this abyss . . . I see the lives for which I lay down my life, peaceful, useful, prosperous and happy . . . I see that I hold a sanctuary in their hearts and in the hearts of their descendants, generations hence. It is a far, far better thing that I do, than I have ever done; it is a far, far better rest that I go to than I have ever known."

COMMENT: And so the life of Sydney Carton achieves the grandeur and promise that had eluded him for so long. In this supreme sacrifice for a woman he loved, Sydney Carton finds a place in the hearts of these people he knew, is finally loved and respected as he had never been before. And they will tell his story for generations to come. So ends "A Tale of Two Cities."

CHARACTER ANALYSES

LUCIE MANETTE.   Lucie Manette is only seventeen years old when we first meet her. She cannot remember her father, who was snatched away from her when she was but a child, and her mother died shortly after. Since then she has been raised by Miss Pross, a kind, loving governess and friend. But despite her unfortunate childhood, Lucie strikes us immediately as a gentle, unassuming young woman with great inner strength. Mr. Lorry, who has not seen her since she was a child, is struck by Lucie's great beauty, modesty and poise when he meets her at Dover. Although Mr. Lorry's news about her father momentarily causes her to lose her composure, she soon recovers and announces her determination to nurse her father back to health and happiness, and she never wavers from this aim during the course of the story. When the doubts in her father's mind awaken old memories, she is there to comfort and steady him.

It is amazing that Lucie has so much influence on so many people in "A Tale of Two Cities," influence which exerts its power although Lucie herself does not consciously use it. Her father depends entirely on her for his physical and emotional well-being. Both Darnay and Carton fall in love with her. Darnay is the man lucky enough to win her, but Carton, though unsuccessful as a suitor (if one may call him unsuccessful who never attempted to be a suitor), still receives spiritual sustenance from Lucie. Even the boorish Mr. Stryver is affected by her beauty and charm, so much so that he even considers marrying her (her powers must indeed be great if a vulgarian such as Stryver could even entertain such a notion). Mr. Lorry looks upon Lucie as the daughter he never had, and Miss Pross' world revolves around her "Ladybird." Even Ernest Defarge's heart is softened by Lucie's tender compassion for her father. In fact, everyone with whom Lucie comes in contact is subtly changed and softened by Lucie's wonderful power. Everyone, that is, except Madame Defarge: Lucie's tearful pleadings can do nothing with that heart of stone.

When Lucie learns of her husband's imprisonment she rushes to Paris to be with him, disregarding the danger. Her behavior during Charles Darnay's long incarceration and trial bear out our first impression: Lucie is a loving, faithful wife who shows strength and determination during the awful months of fear and uncertainty, and her image never dims from the beginning of the book to the end.

CHARLES DARNAY.   Darnay, like his wife Lucie, is a thoroughly good person. This characteristic is made evident as early as his first trial, where, though his life hangs in the balance, he is concerned only about the suffering he is causing Lucie in the testimony she is giving to the court. But his goodness does not prevent him from placing himself in very difficult situations; indeed, it actually seems to be the cause of his difficulties. His insistence on making reparations for the crimes committed by his family causes his uncle, the Marquis, to seek to rid himself of this great nuisance of a nephew , and he almost succeeds in doing so when Darnay is put on trial as a spy for France against England. And later, when he receives Gabelle's letter, Darnay returns to France, in all innocence, to save him, really believing that his good intentions will be recognized by the bloodthirsty populace. He continues to believe this, in his naive manner, even after he is arrested and threatened.

Darnay is a pivotal character in the novel. He serves as a link tying together several threads: Dr. Manette's imprisonment; Madame Defarge's desire for vengeance; and Sydney Carton's ultimate sacrifice. But because of his rather bland personality and his serving as a touchstone for other, greater events, Darnay does not, to any great extent, awaken sympathy in the reader as to his ultimate fate. He tends to merge into the background while other, more distinctive, personalities remain in one's mind.

SYDNEY CARTON.   Sydney Carton is a paradoxical character. His manner is careless, his appearance slovenly; yet, he is the first one to see Lucie faint at Darnay's trial and call assistance. He claims to care for no man; yet, he trades his life for Darnay's.

Carton is revealed as a man of obvious intelligence and ability who, if he applied himself, could probably attain any goal he wished. But he is unable to do so, and so he remains a mental drudge, the unheralded jackal of Stryver's who enables that pompous oaf to get ahead in life while Carton remains in the shadows — a debauched, uncaring fellow. We are told that even at school Carton did other students' work while neglecting his own, and he continues in the same role in working for Stryver. We are not told what he has worked at before teaming up with Stryver, but this relationship seems to fill a need for Carton; for we have the feeling that if his life had not been cut short he would have continued being Stryver's jackal till the end of his days.

Carton is the most real character to the modern reader of "A Tale of Two Cities." First, because he is portrayed "warts and all," that is, his faults are acknowledged and presented as part of his total image, whereas several other characters in the story seem altogether too perfect to be human beings. And second, because his sickness seems such a curiously modern one, one which the French would term a "malaise" and the Germans "Weltschmerz," a world weariness, a disgust with life. For who does not know someone very much like Sydney Carton — intelligent, talented, quick, — who somehow has not been able to achieve his potential and who wanders through life in a kind of alcoholic daze. When he meets Lucie Manette, Carton, for a brief moment, feels that there is still hope, that he can still redeem himself and patch up his life. But only for a moment, for he soon realizes that it is a hopeless dream. Only at the end of the book, when he gives up his life for Darnay's, does he achieve something, does he give his wasted life meaning, and attain a place in the hearts of those who know him, a place that he had searched for so long and so unsuccessfully.

DR. ALEXANDRE MANETTE. Dr. Manette is one of Dickens' most sympathetically drawn characters. When we first meet him he has just been released from the Bastille and he is a mere shell of a man, both physically and emotionally. Beginning his medical career in Paris, he was just starting to make a name for himself, but, through a trick of fate, his career was cut short when he was summoned to a lonely house by two brothers and shortly thereafter imprisoned, without accusations or opportunity to defend himself (see Book the Third — Chapter 10). Locked in a solitary cell for eighteen years, he maintains his shreds of sanity by taking up the trade of shoemaker and it is in this guise that we first meet him.

During the ensuing years, Lucie's loving care restores him to his former self and it seems that he has conquered his old doubts and fears. However, the appearance of Charles Darnay on the scene awakens them again, and finally, on Lucie's wedding day when Charles reveals his true identity, Dr. Manette's carefully built-up strength and emotional stability are wrecked again in a moment and once again he is the helpless shoemaker.

Despite this momentary setback, the Doctor recovers and shows his great strength of character by not revealing to anyone the details of his imprisonment by Darnay's father and uncle. He places his daughter's happiness before all else and keeps silent. His now-found strength is put to the test in Paris after Darnay's arrest. Here Dr. Manette really, comes into his own. He gains strength daily and takes charge of the situation, using his influence over a long, arduous period to finally effect the release of Charles Darnay. But with all his strength of character and good will there is too much working against him and the re-arrest of Darnay and the reading of Dr. Manette's old diary shake the uncertain foundations of his strength and once again the cloud descends and he is the shoemaker — "One Hundred and Five, North Tower." A touching and warm portrait of a noble man.

MR. STRYVER. Mr. Stryver is the product of Dickens' dislike for men who devoted themselves to politics or the law. He regarded them all as a pompous, comic lot and Mr. Stryver fits the image. Stryver is one of those fortunate men who knows what he wants and knows how to go about getting it, but who is so wrapped up in this pursuit that he is completely unaware of anything else. The scene in which Stryver decides that he will give Lucie the honor of having him for a husband gives a wonderful portrait of a gross, self-important man who is totally unable to see himself for what he is, but who manages to convince himself that everyone else is out of step, while he is able to see everything as it really is. A thoroughly obnoxious fellow.

THE DEFARGES. Ernest Defarge is basically a good man who has seen much sadness and injustice about him and who has determined that he will one day set matters to rights. The description of him as "good-humoured looking on the whole, but implacable-looking, too," well suits him, for when the Revolution is set in motion he is its mainspring. Only Lucie and Dr. Manette stir his compassion, and for a moment we feel that even Darnay will be able to enlist his aid; but no, for Defarge shakes off his momentary meakness, refuses to help Darnay, and goes off to fight for the Republic.

Implacable though he may be, Defarge pales beside his wife. Madame Defarge has something of the avenging angel about her. Though she is more than once called a great patriot by her fellows, she is nothing of the sort. Defarge *is* a great patriot, for he is truly caught up by the Revolution and the desire to correct the abuses which have existed for so long. But for Madame Defarge the Revolution is a handy excuse for avenging herself on those who destroyed her family. This is what she has set her mind to and it is the thought of this revenge that has kept her going for so long. When the day finally comes, her terrible anger has so mounted that she joins in the killing with a will, making do with other victims until the true object of her hatred should fall beneath her steely gaze. And though Darnay escapes once, Madame Defarge is not so easily shaken off. When he is condemned at his second hearing, her joy knows no bounds. But this momentary success is not sufficient, for she is soon seeking more heads for the guillotine: Lucie, little Lucie, and Dr. Manette. This is not to be, however, for she encounters Miss Pross and her career is ended before her thirst for blood is slaked. One feels that even if Madame Defarge had succeeded in adding these three to her list of condemned, she would still not have been satisfied and would have spent her life seeking more victims to feed that gnawing hunger for revenge, a hunger that would never be eased.

MISS PROSS. Miss Pross is the typical down-to-earth, no-nonsense, English governess. She is good-hearted and decent, despite an outward gruffness. She has found her place in life as Lucie's maid and she fusses over Lucie as if she were her own. For her Ladybird, Miss Pross would do anything, which she proves in her encounter with Madame Defarge. Up until this encounter Miss Pross has always seen the good in everybody, even in her worthless brother Solomon, from whom she asks only a kind word, despite his mistreatment of her. But even without understanding Madame Defarge's words, her intuition tells Miss Pross that this is a thoroughly evil woman, bent on destroying everything that Miss Pross holds dear, and this belief gives Miss Pross the strength to conquer her adversary.

JERRY CRUNCHER. Jerry Cruncher, odd-job man at Tellson's and "resurrectionist" on the side, is the closest we come to one of Dickens' comic characters. Jerry is not terribly funny, but he is nevertheless a light touch in the otherwise serious-toned novel. But even Jerry is given his part to perform in the plot and the otherwise comic chapters which deal with him turn out to have a great deal of significance in events which occur later.

JARVIS LORRY. Mr. Lorry, though at no time does he seem to be a terribly important character in himself, actually has a great deal to do with the development of the plot. It is he who tells Lucie about her father and goes with her to France to bring him back to England; it is he who brought Lucie from France originally; it is he who gives Darnay the fateful letter which draws him to Paris; and it is he to whom Carton turns to carry out part of the scheme to rescue Darnay. Actually, at most of the crucial turnings of the plot, Mr. Lorry is present and participating. The man of business, who once describes himself as a "mere machine," several times serves as a machine to advance the plot. But Dickens' skill covers the mechanics of development and we think of Mr. Lorry not as a mechanism, but as a warm, cherubic man of affairs who is loved and respected by all those who come in contact with him in the book.

CRITICAL COMMENTARY

INFLUENCE OF CARLYLE. The inspiration for the writing of "A Tale of Two Cities" came from Thomas Carlyle, the great Scottish historian and essayist. Dickens, like so many of his fellow countrymen, had been overwhelmed by Carlyle's book, "The French Revolution," and he kept it within easy reach on his bedside table. With the exception of a small volume, Mercier's "Tableau de Paris," all of Dickens' historical knowledge of the French Revolution and of the city of Paris during the Revolution came from Carlyle. According to Kitton (see bibliography), Dickens, "in order to be accurate in writing 'A Tale of Two Cities' asked Carlyle to lend him some of the authorities quoted in 'The French

Revolution." Carlyle, as a joke, sent all his reference volumes, comprising about two cart-loads of books." We are told that Dickens read them faithfully.

Dickens and Carlyle were quite different types: Carlyle, a noted scholar, collecting and sifting many documents to produce his great work; Dickens, a badly educated man who gathered his material through carefully observing the people and events about him. It was Dickens' genius that he could write about a city and an event about which he knew next to nothing and produce such a stirring, believable portrait of the time. Dickens was well aware that the condition of the peasants was not as bad on the eve of the Revolution as it had been earlier in the century. But taxes were still inequitable (the nobility and clergy were exempt) and the nobles were even trying to revive feudal dues that had lapsed. Carlyle carefully analyzed the first stirrings which led to the eruption years later and the theory of historical inevitability is closely bound up with his name: given a certain set of circumstances, certain results can be predicted, as in the case of the abuses which led to the Revolution. But Carlyle, as he writes, stands aloof from the whirlpool, and one feels that if he had lived at the time he would have protested against the abuses and left it at that. Whereas we have the feeling as we read "A Tale of Two Cities" that Dickens, a man who believed passionately in eradicating any social injustice he came upon, would have joined the mob and stormed the Bastille.

NEW STYLE OF WRITING. In writing "A Tale of Two Cities," Dickens employed a style quite different from that which he had used for his earlier novels. In the earlier works there is a profusion of characters and incidents; here the characters and incidents are few and each event is included in the story because it must be there and each event has a definite place in the structure of the plot. There is no leisurely rambling in the writing, no irrelevant details, nothing episodic. The writing is tight, concentrated, and stripped of all inessential material.

Thus, "A Tale of Two Cities" is a novel of plot rather than character. The characters are ruled by the plot, not the other way around. Even the seemingly unimportant sections concerning Jerry Cruncher or Miss Pross turn out to have a direct bearing on the story. The emphasis is on narrative rather than dialogue. This makes for a gripping tale, one that holds the reader's interest until the last page. But in using this technique, an author assumes the risk of having his characters appear lifeless and lacking in individuality. And in "A Tale of Two Cities" Dickens does not always avoid this pitfall.

CRITICISM OF CHARACTERS. Charles Darnay is a mere shadow of a character. He is a good-hearted, responsible, loving husband and father, but he never assumes a real three-dimentional form. Lucie suffers from the same complaint. She is the conventional pretty heroine, a good daughter, wife, and mother (an ingenue, as Edgar Johnson calls her [see bibliography]), but she has no distinctive personality. Stryver, though he is on stage for only a short while, is well sketched. Dickens always regarded men in politics or law with a jaundiced eye and Stryver conforms to Dickens' image: an insensitive, pushing vulgarian who forges ahead in a world that Sydney Carton can make no sense of or get along in. Jarvis Lorry emerges in a few strokes as a rather distinctive character. Madame Defarge is bloodless, like Lucie and Charles, but for a different reason: she is a cold, vengeful machine seeking to destroy all before her. She remains one of Dickens' most marvelous creations.

Of the other two major male characters, there exists some difference of opinion. Edgar Johnson finds that Dr. Manette, "though sharply and penetratingly observed, is but an outline in comparison with, say, Mr. Dorrit [in "Little Dorrit] who is so subtly and sensitively developed." He finds it "rather evident" that Dickens identified himself most with Sydney Carton, for Dickens, in his own life, searched for love, warmth, and understanding and despaired of ever finding it. Carton, the suffering and heroic soul who feels within himself a deep sense of guilt and remorse and the need for atoning for his sins, attains this love, warmth, and understanding, though he must become a martyr to do it. Kitton, too, states that Dickens had a particular liking for Sydney Carton and he quotes the American writer, Richard Grant White, as having said that "there is not a grander and lovelier figure in literature or history." K. J. Fielding (see bibliography) feels that Dr. Manette is the character that Dickens felt closest to, both because he was an "imprisoned" figure (as Dickens was imprisoned in his domestic situation) and because, like Dickens, Dr. Manette, when in despair, felt a compulsive need for action, for it was "the character of his mind to be always in singular need of occupation."

SIGNIFICANCE OF SUBJECT MATTER. Some critics have believed that there was a great political significance in Dickens' writing a novel about the French Revolution, as a fully-developed work of social protest, elements of which has appeared in earlier novels. But Dickens, though he probably believed in the possibility of an uprising in England, stuck to the main theme of the story and avoided the obvious parallels that he might have used if he had an axe to grind in writing this novel. The significance of the novel as a whole is too great to try to find personal opinions in it, either of Dickens or Carlyle. In any case, as Mr. Johnson points out, the conflict between love and hate, between revolution and sacrifice, in the end gives Carton's martyrdom a personal grandeur that takes away from the social criticism of the story, and, despite its power, half destroys its revolutionary significance.

NOVEL'S LACK OF HUMOR. A criticism frequently made against "A Tale of Two Cities" is that it lacks humor. No one can deny the truth of the statement but it does not seem to be a legitimate complaint. True, humor is an obvious component of most of Dickens' other novels and many of Dickens' greatest creations are comic characters. It does not necessarily follow, however, that therefore there should be some great comic characters in "A Tale of Two Cities." Strong humor would be out of place in this story. And, though Jerry Cruncher and Miss Pross do add a leavening of humor to the serious tone of the book, no one can legitimately state that Dickens intended them to be funnier than they turned out to be but failed in his intentions. Ironically, those people who have not read Dickens enjoy "A Tale of Two Cities" most, while ardent Dickens advocates are disappointed with it as compared to his other works, largely because of the missing element of humor. This lack of humor was particularly objected to by Gissing (see bibliography), a noted Dickens authority. He writes, " 'A Tale of Two Cities' is not characteristic of Dickens in anything but theme (the attack on social tyranny). With humour lacking we feel the restraint throughout." In the end, the book "leaves no strong impression on the mind; even the figure of Carton grows dim against a dimmer background."

POINTS OF STYLE. Dickens is a story-teller, first and foremost. He was always so in his novels and is particularly so in "A Tale of Two Cities." Here the story is the thing, and his style is subordinated to it. He is often verbose and redundant. His mannerisms sometime become grossly apparent — for example, instead of saying, "He was christened Jerry," he says, "On the youthful occasion of his renouncing by proxy the works of darkness he had received the added appellation of Jerry." But his style has vigor, clearness, soundnes of construction. Dickens was a master of the English language; his prose is finished, well-chosen, and idiomatic. His landscape drawing is very fine: the description of the village and the chateau is very slight but singularly vivid and complete. He is a master of imagery: stone faces, blood-red fountain, crimson dawn, blue flies searching for carrion, a golden thread, spectre-white dust covering the figure under the Marquis' coach — all these help to fuse and concentrate the novel's themes and incidents.

Dickens was a master of description. To quote Gissing, "Dickens had easy graphic power, wonderfully minute observation. His literary method is that of all the great novelists. To set before his reader the image so vivid in his own mind, he simply describes and reports. We have, in general, a very precise and complete picture of externals — the face, the gesture, the habit. In this Dickens excels; he proves to us by sheer force of visible detail, how actual was the mental form from which he drew. We learn the tone of voice, the trick of utterance; he declared that every word spoken by his characters was audible to him. Then does the man reveal himself in colloquy; sometimes once for all, sometimes by degree, in chapter after chapter — though this is seldom the case. We know these people because we see and hear them."

"SENTIMENTALITY" IN WRITING.   Two other frequent criticisms of the book that we should touch on here are: 1. the sometimes unbearable sentimentality, and; 2. the over-frequent use of coincidence in the working out of the plot. The first is a complaint often heard, with much justice. Both Edgar Johnson and K. J. Fielding single out the garret scene where Lucie Manette first sees her father after his release from the Bastille. In Fielding's words, "the scene seems derivative and conventional. Though excellent theater, the dialogue too often has many of the pretentious faults of Victorian drama: just when it ought to carry emotional depth and conflict it begins strumming on stock phrases until released by action." And Johnson: "the scene is marred by the literary artifice of Lucie's tearful rhythmic expressions, 'Weep for it, weep for it'." The criticism is a just one, particularly of this one scene which probably even the most romantic reader would find hard to swallow. Johnson's statement that Carton's death is, for many readers, "drenched in over-indulged sentiment," is probably an exaggeration. It has quite a different mood from the garret scene and, somehow, words that in other circumstances would seem mawkish, here attain a splendor and nobility, and the closing segment is, as it was meant to be, the most affecting part of the book.

USE OF COINCIDENCE.   The second criticism, concerning the use of coincidence, is, if one considers it logically, a legitimate one, and if one were to read the novel's many coincidences strung out like a necklace — Defarge, leader of the Revolution and former servant of Dr. Manette; Madame Defarge, the younger sister of the doomed pair killed by the Saint Evrémonde and wife of Ernest Defarge; Darnay's return to Paris, and danger, from a safe haven in London; Defarge's discovery of Dr. Manette's diary intact when a similarly unearthed paper had crumbled to dust; Barsad, Miss Pross' long-lost brother, turning up in Paris; and, finally, Carton's looking so much like Darnay that a switch is made without being detected — certainly all of them are a lot to swallow in one gulp. But somehow they get by in the context of the story, and Dickens' skill sees to it that we don't pause as we come to each one and consider its legitimacy before we continue reading. Instead, they all appear in their proper places and they seem quite right and natural when they do appear.

SUMMARY.   "A Tale of Two Cities" is, in Stephan Leacock's words, "a great book despite its inperfections." It has been read and enjoyed by millions of people during the one hundred and five years of its existence, and it will doubtless continue to be one of Dickens' most popular novels for many years to come. For, though critics may point out any number of technical imperfections in the book, the power of the narrative is such that even the most laconic reader cannot fail to be caught up in it. And, after all, this is what an author sets out to do. It cannot be denied that Dickens has accomplished this aim brilliantly in "A Tale of Two Cities," and thus it is assured an honored place in the catalogue of Dickens' works.

REVIEW QUESTIONS AND ANSWERS

1. Without having any special knowledge of the French Revolution, do the details used by Dickens ring true?

Like any novelist writing a novel based on an historical event, Dickens could pick and choose among the historical facts, omitting what he wished and even modifying the facts that he did use. Many authors use their poetic license to distort the original facts beyond recognition; this Dickens does not do. The only specific historical event of the Revolution that Dickens employs in "A Tale of Two Cities" is the fall of the Bastille, and in this sketch the dates and description conform to the known facts. In his other historical reference Dickens remains faithful to Carlyle's data.

He has, however, omitted many of the causes of the Revolution (such as the intellectual movement and the writings of the French philosopher, Rousseau) to emphasize the abuses of the nobility as the prime cause of the uprising. This, of course, has great dramatic value though it is not quite accurate. As has been mentioned, the peasants were better off in 1789 than they had been earlier in the century, although abuses still existed. Yet the French Revolution broke out in 1789 and not before. Stanley Loomis (see bibliography) states that "an ill-administered, ineffectual tyranny induces a climate hospitable to ideas in which are planted and nourished the seeds that grow into revolution." In other words, a stronger tyranny would have prevented an uprising. The fact that the nobility was not able to grind down the peasantry under a heavy heel is what led to the nourishment of revolutionary ideas.

Dickens also omits the leading figures of the Revolution, such as Marat, Danton, and Robespierre, but this is a legitimate novelistic approach and one need not quarrel with it. The noted British author Bulwer-Lytton thought that the description of the Marquis was historically inaccurate at such a late date, but Dickens defended his description stating that Mercier's "Tableau de Paris" served as the authority for it. Chesterton (see bibliography) goes so far as to state that Dickens' picture of the French Revolution is probably quite a bit more like the real thing than Carlyle's, for, he says, "The French Revolution was a much simpler world than Carlyle could understand; for Carlyle was subtle and not simple. Dickens could understand it, for he was simple and not subtle. He understood that plain rage against plain political injustice; he understood again that obvious vindictiveness and that obvious brutality which followed."

2.   Do the plot and action of the story fulfill the book's title?

London was Dickens' world. He knew nothing about Paris or the rest of Europe; and though he traveled much during his years of success, he remained in outlook a Londoner and he felt that London was the only city he understood. Despite this handicap, Dickens wrote his "Tale of Two Cities" and brilliantly described Paris, a city he did not know: pre-Revolutionary Paris with its squalor, its hordes of downtrodden peasants, its arrogant nobility. As Chesterton says, "his description of the city he did not know is almost better than his description of the city he did know." Perhaps Dickens thought his readers would know London well and so would not be particularly interested in details about that city; or perhaps he felt challenged in writing about Paris. In any case, much of the description and most of the action concerns Paris. Except for the descriptions of the Manette household and Tellson's Bank, of Darnay's trial and Cly's funeral, there is very little about London in the novel. "A Tale of Two Cities" is really a tale of one city; and that city is Paris.

3.   It is never revealed why or how Dr. Manette is released from the Bastille. Discuss the possible explanations for his release.

This is a question that cannot be answered with any certainty. In the opening chapters we learn that Dr. Manette has been released from the Bastille after eighteen years imprisonment and is in the care of Ernest Defarge, his former servant, while awaiting the arrival of Lucie Manette and Jarvis Lorry. Never, during the rest of the novel, are we told why he has been released at this particular time or how Defarge has reentered the picture to take care of his former master. Since there is so little to go on, many explanations are possible but two come to mind which seem more likely than any others. Before the Revolution erupted various concessions were offered by the government to the populace to try to head off an uprising. This is historical fact, though Dickens has made no mention of such concessions in order to enhance his dark portrait of the nobility. It is conceivable that Dr. Manette was released from the Bastille as part of a general amnesty granted political prisoners there; and inasmuch as Dr. Manette had no relatives in Paris, Defarge was the logical person to whom Dr. Manette would be entrusted.

The second possibility is hinted at in certain passages in the book. The present Marquis Saint Evrémonde is out of favor with the court. We learn this in Book Two, Chapters seven and eight, through the coldness shown him at Monseigneur's party and through the conversation with his nephew, Charles Darnay. But we are not told why he is out of favor. It is possible that he fell out of favor when some higher personage discovered the *lettre de cachet,* the one that imprisoned Dr. Manette, and this Lord gave the order for the doctor's release. Or, conversely, it could be that he had fallen out of favor for some other offense and the doctor was released as a sort of slap in the face for the Marquis; as an insult, to make him realize that he was not the all-powerful man he considered himself to be.

4. Why was Dr. Manette summoned by the brothers to tend their victims?

This is another question to which we can give no definite answer. Possibly the idea in the brothers' minds was to call the doctor to administer something to put the dying brother and sister out of their misery, but when they sized up their man, they realized the folly in proposing such a plan to him. It is not likely that they were trying to be merciful in summoning a doctor, for they show no sympathy, only relief, when the two patients die. Perhaps it was their idea to have the doctor there as a witness that they were doing everything they could to save the two, but since they were the cause of the peasants' conditions and since they were sure of their power, this seems unlikely.

Actually, none of the above possibilities stands up under close scrutiny, and we can only conclude that it was a naked, dramatic device to explain many events that took place later, and, as such, it cannot be explained in any logical manner.

5. Most of Dickens' works appeared in serial form initially. Do you feel that the structure of "A Tale of Two Cities" was determined by this factor?

Undoubtedly, "A Tale of Two Cities" was constructed to conform to the requirements of serialization, as it probably could be shown Dickens' other works were. When one is writing a segment of a story for readers, there are several elements which must be present — there must be a certain amount of pathos, a certain amount of humor, a dash of this, a pinch of that, so that the segment will stand as a unity; and the story must be developed in such a way that the reader will want to read the next installment. Hence, the so-called "cliff-hanger" in film serials: as one installment ends the heroine is tied to a railroad track and the 6:20 express is due at any moment. This kind of thing is frequently used by Dickens in "A Tale of Two Cities," though in a much more subtle way. A chapter is closed with some puzzling statement or bit of information which promises to be cleared up in the next installment: for example, Jerry Cruncher's remark, "You'd be in a blazing bad way if recalling to life was to come into fashion, Jerry!" One wonders what significance this has. Or, the words "To be buried alive for eighteen years!" which close Chapter Three. What does it mean? Or, much later, at Darnay's second hearing: "The paper was read, as follows." And there the chapter ends. What red-blooded Englishman would not be waiting at the news vendor's stand the next week when the new issue came out, to learn the contents of Dr. Manette's diary?

6.   Several of the lesser characters are of interest, either for the part they play in the development of the plot or for something inherent in themselves as Dickens has drawn them. Discuss these characters, namely: The Marquis Saint Evrémonde (Darnay's uncle); Gaspard; Jacques Three; the Mender of Roads.

Each of the above-mentioned characters is a representation of a type. As we read a description of one of the above we are given to understand that he is simply one of many, that there are hundreds just like him and his virtues and faults are the virtues and faults of all of the rest.

The **MARQUIS SAINT EVREMONDE,** the uncle of Charles Darnay, is a product of the aristocratic system that prevailed in France for hundreds of years before the Revolution. He is neither better nor worse than any of his noble brethren, and Dickens makes it clear that he could have chosen any one of the noble lords at court and the resulting portrait would have been much like the one of the Marquis Saint Evrémonde. He is handsome, well-dressed, always poised and self-assured; and there is a look of cruelty in his face. He cares for nothing but his own position and pleasures. The death of a child beneath the wheels of his carriage causes him no distress: he is only annoyed because his journey has been delayed. He really believes that Gaspard is at fault for letting his child be run down and the Marquis feels that he is being very beneficient in bestowing a gold coin upon the bereaved father. This coldness and obliviousness is further portrayed in the conversation between the Marquis and Charles Darnay. It is clear that the Marquis would have no compunction in eliminating his nephew if it were in the power to do so, blood ties meaning as little to him as the misery of a father whose child has just been killed.

GASPARD.   We are told almost nothing in the way of physical description about Gaspard: only that he is tall and thin and has a somewhat comic air about him when we first meet him. He utters only a few words, when his child is killed, and he occupies only a very few lines in the book. Yet we remember him; for the image that remains in our mind is an image symbolic of the thousands of oppressed peasants who labor and die to provide for the pleasures of the nobility. This miserable creature is pushed too far and, enraged, he throws off his meek, subservient manner and slays the Marquis. Thus do his fellow citizens throw off their fetters and revenge themselves on their oppressors shortly after Gaspar's desperate act has shown them the way.

JACQUES THREE. Jacques Three, like Gaspard, occupies very little space in the novel but he, too, symbolizes the unrest that lingers among the peasantry, with his nervous hands, and his craving, hungry manner. He gnaws on his fingers constantly and cannot slake the gnawing hunger inside him. The thought of death delights him and when the Evrémonde family is doomed to destruction he says, "Magnificent!" and is beside himself with pleasure. This symbolic hunger for revenge is one which rests in the breasts of all the French populace. In Jacques Three it is more obvious, and thus it points to the bloody massacres ahead in which the intoxication of bloodletting creates the same hungry look on thousands of faces as now exists on the face of Jacques Three.

THE MENDER OF ROADS. The Mender of Roads is an ordinary, insignificant peasant who finds himself a person of some importance through the circumstance of having seen Gaspard beneath the Marquis' carriage. He enjoys this new-found notoriety and tells his story throughout the neighboring villages, embellishing the details. Later, as a member of the Jacquerie, he enjoys an even greater feeling of importance when he tells of Gaspard's execution; and when he is takn to Versailles by the Defarges to see the King and Queen, his pride swells even more. Still later, the transformation is complete. As a wood-sawyer he has achieved stature. He is in the thick of things and never misses a performance by the executioner, enjoying the art of that bloody practitioner in dispatching so many souls in such a short time. This transformation is similar to the one taking place throughout France. Many weak, dull people now belong to something bigger than themselves, yet they feel a direct participation in events. The more blood spilled, the greater they feel their power to be; and this exaltation leads to greater and greater excesses.

BIBLIOGRAPHY AND GUIDE TO FURTHER RESEARCH

"A Tale of Two Cities" is available in a number of editions. It is a volume in the uniform sets of Dickens' works published by the Oxford University Press and St. Martin's Press. In a less expensive cloth edition the novel is available in the Modern Library and in Everyman's Library. These two editions are also available in paperback format, as is the edition published by the new American Library (a Signet paperback).

WORKS ON THE FRENCH REVOLUTION

Burke, Edmund. *Reflections on the French Revolution* (1790). New York: E. P. Dutton, 1910 (Everyman's Library).

Carlyle, Thomas. *The French Revolution* (1837). New York: Random House (The Modern Library).

Depont, M. *Answer to the Reflections of the Right Honorable Edmund Burke*. London: J. Debrett, 1791.

Gregory, Allene. *The French Revolution and the English Novel*. New York: G. P. Putnam's Sons, 1915.

Loomis, Stanley. *Paris in the Terror*. Philadelphia: J. B. Lippincott Co , 1964.

DICKENS AND HIS WORKS

Burton, Richard. *Charles Dickens*. Indianapolis: The Bobbs-Merrill Co., 1919.

Chancellor, Edwin B. *Dickens and His Times*. London: Richards, 1932.

Charles, Edwin. *Some Dickens Women*. London: T. W. Laurie, Ltd., 1926.

Chesterton, G. K. *Appreciations and Criticism of the Works of Charles Dickens*. London: J. M. Dent, 1911.

Chesterton, G. K. *Charles Dickens; a Critical Study*. New York: Dodd, Mead and Co., 1906.

Christian, Mildred G. "Carlyle's Influence Upon the Social Theory of Dickens." *Trollopian* (March 1947).

Christie, O. F. *Dickens and His Age*. London: Heath Cranton, Ltd., 1939.

Cockshut, A. O. J. *The Imagination of Charles Dickens*. London: Collins, 1961.

Crotch, W. W. *The Soul of Dickens*. London: Chapman and Hall, Ltd., 1916.

Fielding, K. J. *Charles Dickens; a Critical Introduction*. New York: Longmans, Green, 1958.

Forster, John. *The Life of Charles Dickens*. Philadelphia: J. B. Lippincott Co., 1872-74.

Gissing, George R. *Critical Studies of the Works of Charles Dickens*. New York: Greenberg, 1924.

Handley, George M. *Notes on Dickens' "A Tale of Two Cities."* London: The Normal Press, 190?.

Johnson, Edgar. *Charles Dickens, His Tragedy and Triumph*. New York: Simon and Schuster, 1952.

Kitton. Frederic G. *Charles Dickens, His Life, Writings, and Personality*. London and Edinburgh: T. C. & E. C. Jack, 1902.

Leacock, Stephen. *Charles Dickens, His Life and Work*. New York: Doubleday and Co., 1934.

Matz. Bertram W. *The Great Victorian Writers: Dickens the Novelist Carlyle the Philosopher*. London: Chapman & Hall, 1905.

Maurois, André. *Dickens*. London: J. Lane, 1934.

Miller. Joseph H. *Charles Dickens, the World of His Novels*. Cambridge Harvard University Press, 1959.